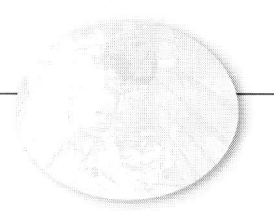

At Maureen's

Bernadette Mayer and Greg Masters

Introduction by Lewis Warsh

Crony Books, New York

©2013 Bernadette Mayer and Greg Masters. All rights reserved.

No part of this book may be reproduced, stored in a retrieval system or transmitted by any means without the written permission of the publisher.

Published by
Crony Books
437 East 12 Street #26
New York, NY 10009
March 2013

Photos by Bernadette Mayer, except where noted

ISBN: 978-0-9859267-1-7

to Maureen Owen

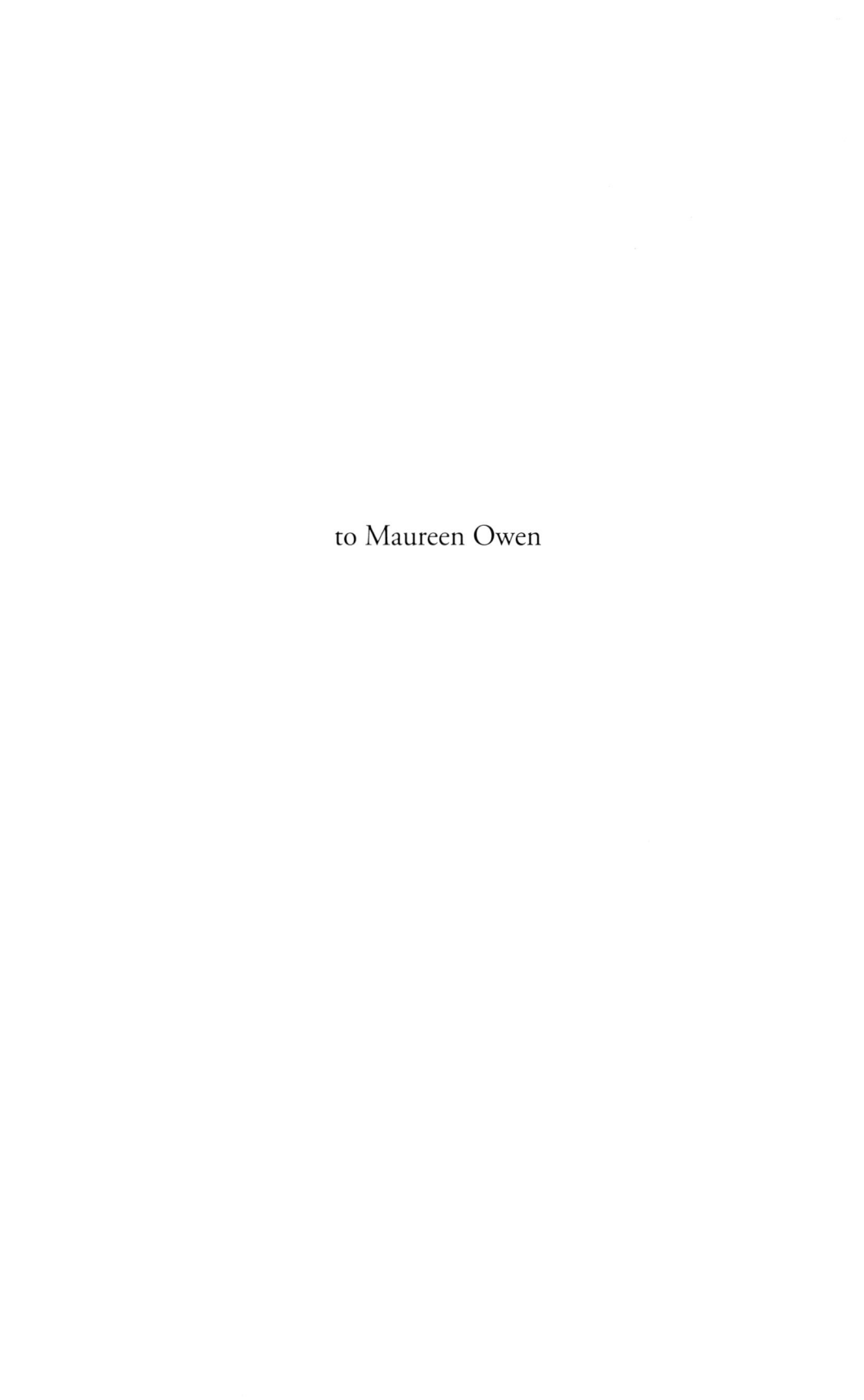

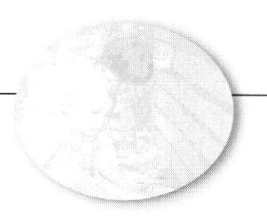

Preface

My friend, the poet and editor Maureen Owen, asked me if I'd like to house sit for her for a month during the summer of 1980 while she, her husband, Ted Mankevich, and three children – Patrick, Ulysses and Kyran – went on vacation. The "job" involved keeping an eye on things, gathering the mail, feeding the pets and watering the plants. Yes, of course, I said immediately.

The house was off a rural road in Guilford, Connecticut, a small community on the Long Island Sound around 15 miles outside of New Haven. To me, after a few years living a bohemian existence in a tenement in the East Village of Manhattan, the saltbox house was quite luxurious with its domestic accoutrements, a barn out back and a raspberry field down the road.

The next summer she offered the house again and, for that second summer, I asked my friends – the poets, writers and editors Bernadette Mayer and Lewis Warsh – if they'd care to join me with their three young children, Marie, Sophia and Max. It didn't occur to me at the time that this might not have been what Maureen intended for her house, and was something I should have gotten her permission to do. So, 30+ years later, I apologize Maureen for my lapse in manners.

At the time, Bernadette was director of the Poetry Project, a literary center housed in St. Mark's Church in the East Village. From reading this journal, we see that she was researching, compiling information and thinking about what would become her book *Utopia* (United Artists Books, 1984). She was also corresponding with Bill Berkson, an eight-year segment of which would eventually take shape as the collaborative book, *What's Your Idea of a Good Time* (Tuumba Press), issued in 2007.

I was at this time an office assistant at the Poetry Project and editor of the *Poetry Project Newsletter*. I was also co-editor, with Michael Scholnick and Gary Lenhart, of *Mag City*, a poetry magazine.

Reading over these pages, it's clear that we put that house to the test, but I think managed to clean up for ourselves. Maybe we replaced Maureen's wine with lesser bottles, what did we know of taste then? And it seems we might have run a radiator hose down on one of the cars at our disposal. But I hope the house was in reasonable enough order for its owners on their return. Come to think of it, I wasn't asked to house sit anymore after that summer.

After a few days there together, Bernadette and I hit upon the idea of keeping a double journal of our stay as a thank you to Maureen. We would keep a daily accounting of the goings on and, at the end of our sojourn, we'd weave each of our day's entries together so as to offer Maureen a *Rashomon*-like narrative of what went on in her house while she was away.

– Greg Masters

*Introduction to the Guilford Journals
of Mayer and Masters*

    I haven't read much of these journals yet, which isn't to say that I don't intend to or that not reading them disqualifies me from writing an introduction. I would have kept a journal of my own during the time we stayed at your house, but I was involved in a (writing) project which involved transcribing journals I wrote in 1962 and 1963 and I was sick of journals – just the idea of keeping a journal made me ill. I have written a few poems since I've been here, and things that happened while we were here and things I've seen will probably pop up in poems for the next few years, at least. The oddest thing about Guilford is the house for migrant workers up the road, and I wish we could stay longer and pick all the great raspberries which will be ripe in about a week – Bernadette and I actually did pick a few on a walk down the road a few nights ago. (I prefer raspberry picking to strawberry picking since you don't have to bend as much and my back has been acting up again.) Actually, I have a pain in my leg too. It was fun to swim in the lake and in the Sound (today we met Quincy Howe at the Sound) and to drive George's car, and to go to The Little Store on the way to the lake and buy beer and sandwiches and pretzels for the kids. Marie learned how to swim and I guess we'll have to join the Y in New York so she can continue practicing. I'm not looking forward to going back to New York, I must admit. I've never read any of the Tolkien books so it was odd to work in a room surrounded by Tolkien paraphernalia, but it was a pleasure to begin work early in the evening when it was still light and look out the window until it got dark, and drink coffee. We had fun here. It feels like we just arrived yesterday. Most nights I'd stop work at about 11:30 and meet Greg in the living room and we'd watch television or look for something to watch while Bernadette typed her journal, Greg had already finished his, then Bernadette would join us and we'd either drink a whisky, a beer, some wine or eat ice cream or lettuce and tomato sandwiches, depending on our moods. Then we'd go off to bed. The first few nights here, I had trouble sleeping, but after we began going to the beach regularly and swimming, I had no problems. So I guess what they say about getting proper exercise is probably true. I hope you had a good time too on your travels.

                                                                                    Love,
                                                                                    Lewis

                                                                                    P.S. What's Stacy's last name?

June 21

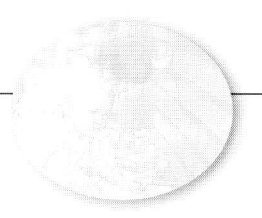

It's nice to be here there are so many things and machines too, this orator is impressive, so far we've seen a woodchuck, millions of gypsy caterpillars, the gypsy cold something tea, Chaffinch Island, a miniscule camera, sidecars, bluejays of course, the rabbit and horses, the cats, I have a lot of work to do but I don't know how to begin to do it, first or while I have to read all the Utopian books, then simultaneously type out the less-than-Utopian journal, all the while interspersing the stuff from the books, today. We went to Finast's, it was freezing, I was still wet from swimming, Max rode in the cart, we bought chickens, fruits and vegetables, diapers, coffee and paper towels and peanut butter and oatmeal bread. At Chaffinch Island the tide was coming high at 2:10 so while we were there the water when the boats made waves pushed up onto the little hummock we were on, Maureen, you use a very old Webster's, your room is beautiful. So the waves were threatening to among other things wash Lewis's glasses away. The children went to bed much more quickly than last night but Sophia still keeps asking when all the other people are coming back, where they are, and when we are going home. Greg is very gregarious (pertaining to community or colony), this orator is peculiar. The strawberry fields, we must make something. After swimming in the salt water for the first time in ten years I think, I ate a leftover anchovy. We talked about everyone we know, Grace called her father, Greg his and Lewis his to wish a good Father's Day. Grace and I decided that Ted's shed was an ideal model for the perfect psychiatrist's office, except for those patients who need to pace. Grace noticed a book called *The Psychology of Computer Programming*, it was red. Sitting in the shed with Grace and Marie, Marie made some some numbers and hung them up, she found some papaya and honey candy and ate it. This orator hunts I mean hurts my eyes. We heard an owl this morning, me and Marie. The sidecars were very good. *The Intimate Journal* by George Sand looks great, as does *The Haunted Pool*. I wish we had a nanny so I could just work and read for at least ten hours of every day. It's shocking that the phone doesn't ring, except that Bob called to say that Russ Little's release from jail prevents him from staying in San Francisco, so he's going to go on to San Diego to tape the Paul Blackburn archive. Lewis seems calmer. In a way I wish it were winter so we really could do nothing but read. Yet something still makes me prefer or choose writing to reading, I think it has to do with the children. Summer solstice, the caterpillars fall on your head, it was hot and sunny till late afternoon, it rained at evening, now it's cloudy, can't see any stars, the horse is huge, it astonishes me to think of the enormous horse in the barn at night, as if I went to see the animal at midnight, it would be like a vision. Lewis is working just above me in Ulysses's room and Greg has chosen to sleep and work in the shed, though he's been reading in the house all night, and now he and Lewis are conversing in the kitchen, they read the *NY Times*

today and the pope has a fever. Greg and Lewis came in and we talked about the books on the shelves. I'll make a July calendar and go to read, the house is so big, I heard a child cry and, as has been my habit in the city, first thought it must be someone else's child. Tomorrow is another evening. Load camera with generous gift of film. I wonder if I'll dream again a long play in rhyming couplets ending, unfinished, with the word "turtle." And long dreams about Poetry Project business. Now I sit by a window in the country in a room almost of my own which is all I've ever wanted, what a pleasure. Had chicken, potatoes, corn, stuffing and salad for dinner. Just like in a book.

Farm Hands
on a picture of Maureen and Ted's house

a place is not a mirror
a plant is not a man or life since photography
now the trees have got back up around the house
and we're entitled to have everything now
we've survived our own pioneer days
and with catholicity we erase the memory
off a part of the house that doesn't exist
in favor of the freedom like horses
of men and women exchanging houses
full of loose, metaphorical and magical things
not necessarily consequent to order and use
but better for wellbeing and scarce inspiration
that the dedication of the old road of mud
haunted as the notice of old feelings
less much than you might expect and not mean,
the treeless life of drinking from a pitcher
& pouring carefully from the manual cup of
still poetry like a disastrous fire
in a well-known well full of compost
on the slanted property of an athlete's poetry
Sweet tea we Utopia from communitas or something we ate
a whole lot of Strunk and White in association with the coyote
& sense smoke filled the personality of Greg and Lewis and
six film scripts were proteanly master-minded in our world
warlike dreams of Murphy's Law, Mankevich's razor and plain old
Connecticut hodge-podge-ism alone and alive till your collected
poems dove out to a man to a woman like children divesting
their stuff at the pump to cool off and have some thrills, in
this case the astonishment, having recollected the gigantic
horse and taken in the notion of gargantuan pee and shit, of

getting as cold as you can for the sake of being cool out of
exuberance for bananas and other suckling fruits all day long,
lucky as a telephone, antique as a leafy old tree, sprightly
as one of the many Lepidoptera in its deathless prime.

June 22

    Woke up, Sophia was telling Marie was gone and she was, had gone to disturb Greg who slept while Marie was drawing in the shed. I got mad that Marie would wander out and off. Had pancakes and sausages and went to Guilford which is very expensive and looks like Southampton, a ream of paper is $9.95. Got pads, raw milk, pails and shovels, wrapping paper and stamps, spent about $20, Lewis drove George's car. Then we went to the town beach which is beautiful and full of only women and children, Lewis was the only man, Greg didn't come. Found the fish store, got scratched by barnacles yesterday, saw a jellyfish today, Max got too sunburned, now he's fussing, Sophia had a few tantrums but mostly she and Marie play Dick and Mary and tell us how they're married and going camping which they do up on the hill where they hit stones with sticks and why do babies cry, you can actually hear the child next door crying sometimes. The horse went riding today with a young woman driving a Mercedes-Benz, night seems to come early here. We're out of horse feed and they don't answer. Greg got a postcard, maybe Max will stop crying, Greg went upstairs with the Balmex to rub some on Max's arms to see if that'll make him feel better. It seemed like it would rain today but was hot and sunny all day. The kids loved the horse swings at the beach playground, I did too. Everything is horses. The horsewoman wore a plastic helmet, Greg just called to see if I had any Ko-Rec-Type. Lewis got caterpillars in his hair. Max stopped crying, now he's started again. I have to call Steve to tell him the gerbil's still at our house. We gave the rabbit the rest of the spinach and beet greens, Greg is reading the Olive Schreiner book and *New York Hat Line,* which I'd never seen. A beautiful picture of Mount Rainier on the front page of the *Times,* we listened to Philip Glass's record and played the piano, Maureen and Ted have practically everything – country, ocean, home and the means to support it and nearness to city and they're not crazy either, I'll bet there's a lot of people in the world who have such a desirable life, but maybe not many who are "o.k." Now Max has stopped crying, the main Utopian issues seem to be money and pleasure. Funny that I'll get to write this book about Utopias in such a Utopia (Sophia: "I want to go nowhere"). Heard and saw fantastic birds today, including what looked like a starling at the Sound.

    In fact when I consider any social system that prevails in the modern world, I can't, so help me God, see it as anything but a conspiracy of the rich to advance their own interests under pretext of organizing society.

                                                                – Thomas More

June 23

It'd be nice if New York was in Guilford, Connecticut, and that means Poetry Project too. Woke up with dreams of a giant benefit for the Project featuring the Muppets (not a bad idea) the dream was mainly about complications about seating arrangements and social surrounding occasions – all caused though by Greg's postcard from Chris. It's hilarious that just as I was never alone in New York except to go to the Poetry Project (where I was never alone), here I am never alone except to be in Maureen's room and work at her magical typewriter. Took all three children downstairs at once this morning and suggested to Lewis that he sleep late, he couldn't sleep last night, but he got up too soon anyway and we made different breakfasts for everybody (have to replenish the popular Raisin Bran), and seemed to deal with breakfast, horse, cats and lying about, for hours till we went back again to the town beach. Unthreatening clouds covered the sky and this time absolutely no one was in the water. Eventually I went in and it made me warm instead of cold. Marie and I collected shells, all the children and I dug a deep hole which Max fell into, Greg and Lewis read newspapers and books, we had beer and crackers, juice and oranges, then we went home. Greg said the afternoon was too sunny. We ate pasta with the leftover pesto for dinner. Marie can jump rope over 32 times in a row, and can do all sorts of athletic variations on it, today she started clapping her hands with the jump rope in them in between jumps. Are those trees Huckleberry? Mulberry? What is Checkerberry Syrup? What's it for? Greg said he might be feeling too selfish to have children, to devote so much energy to. When we fix food Greg says, "Oh, another meal." It's true the meals come too quickly for grownups. Lewis and Greg talk, I feel mortal and heavy, Sophia discovers "I games" in Patrick's room, Lewis says Maureen should write her autobiography, Greg is reading Lewis's novel, I am telling everyone who Edward Bellamy is. Spoke to Steve last night and to Morris Golde today who got a grant of $250 for the Poetry Project, wrote letters of thanking. Bought two loaves of white bread from the bakery. Lewis bought Jack Daniels and had two drinks. There's some plan to watch *The Shining* on TV.

June 24

Watched *The Shining* last night, it was awful, axes go into people's chests and creepy, stayed up late and then this morning went back to the beach, it was low tide, ate sandwiches at a fast food place called Roy Rogers and went and made Vichyssoise, had that and ice cream for dinner, watched *Close Encounters of the Third Kind* and *The Jerk*, I feel entirely different today than I did yesterday. *The Shining*'s an analogy to family life. Caterpillars fall on our heads in the living room and under the trees. Greg asked what shells are made of and what is hibiscus (from Sandy's poem). Lewis tried to jump rope. That's all that happened. Max drank bubble solution.

June 25

    Long days and nights though the days seem to end more quickly than in the city, that is, get dark. It rains and we spend a day wandering about, thunder and lightning and everything heightening, that's what little girls are made of. We finally went out in the midst of the heaviest rain late in the afternoon to go to the library which is full of generous services, I took out a book on Utopian communities in California, Lewis took *Appointment in Samarra* by John O'Hara and Greg bought a Robert Herrick book and took out two others which I didn't see and the children took out one book each. Turns out we went to the supermarket then, Finast, to buy spaghetti, sauce, and oh the rest of our shopping list which wouldn't interest anyone, the children ate three free bananas while we were there. I thought of two good titles which I'd seen: "Eels on toast points" and "Shoreline Mental Health." We ate our usual sumptuous meal and lingered too long in the garden afterwards – Marie and Sophia were in bed but Max was still up – we spoke of the Poetry Project and other things, then I put Max to bed while reading *Looking Backward* (Max refused to nurse when he woke up this morning for the first time in his 1-1/2 years!), then Suki wafted in, just back from Cambridge where she was with her mother who's in the hospital. Suki is fun to talk to because she changes so much while she is talking. Then Lewis convinced me that I must watch at least the last half-hour of *Urban Cowboy* but I couldn't stand it when there was this scene where the cowboy was beating up his girlfriend and shouting at her to pick something up and then fix him some food. It reminded me of Michael Brownstein. I thought it was much worse watching this than even *The Shining*. I said to Lewis and Greg, who left at that point, we have enough emotion in our own lives, we surely don't need these movies. An inane thing to say. The odd thing about *Looking Backward* is that it's hard to remember it was written in 1888 with a view to 2000 as "utopia," seeing as how 1981 is much less than that. Greg got a beautiful shirt today from Chris with decals of roses ironed on, he looked quite spiffy in the supermarket, and of course, everywhere else. Marie jumped and jumped some more, she can jump rope more than 50 times now and if you try that yourself, you'd be amazed at how hard it is. Sophia and Marie fought a lot today but they liked the library and Max ate dinner for the first time from a real chair. He liked it but was still very demanding and wants everything on the table for his own. Marie and I did exercises after dinner. Why do I tremble? Now it is thunderstorming again, for a while the lights flickered earlier in the day, then after dinner the sun came out and we welcomed it, now another storm like the great fast clouds in the space movies. Got a letter from Russell today. Suki says he's "living with somebody"! Peggy called but Lewis couldn't hear her so she's supposed to call back but I think I'll call her. After that I'd planned to type out another day in my journal but perhaps not, the rain smells wonderful and this is what I was wishing for – a rain in the country. Did I tell you that yesterday I got to use the Cuisinart to make the Vichyssoise, which we ate cold today. Can I say I would like to be no one in no-land, then that is just a wish for utopia, noman or nowoman has ever seen. Stephanie, who turns out to be Suki's cousin, daughter of Quincy Howe, didn't come to take the children for a pony ride today because of the rain, perhaps soon. Maybe tomorrow or the next day Suki will lead us to both the lake and the book farm. We told her about Simon's arrival to the neighborhood. Sweet peace, I did my exercises this morning in Ulysses' room, my foot still hurts from the barnacles and today Lewis stepped on a tack and screamed so loud both Greg and I thought he had had another back episode. Then we told him he dare not scream in that way so as to scare us. We talk with Greg about rich and poor and this evening a bit about Catholicism. I'll call Peggy.

    Truly if I wrote what I really thought it would be unprintable. I would love to be a person who is just involved with her thoughts and much blank intellectuality so I could just be an intellectual because after all one takes so much crap for being one anyway and hardly anybody in the world can read one's works anyway that to be so specialized or something seems odd (unless I can write a great book about utopias that everybody can read, but I could probably only write it and only not write it if I could be relieved of taking care of my children, or not relieved of that daily exigency, it would indeed be nice to be able to work full-time) anyway I lost my thought which was to be intellectual in this America is weird enough without also having the burden of a great emotional life which is all put on, I mean it is all a burden we've been led to believe in, that it could happen, that we all could be so involved with ourselves and with our desires which are wonderful. I must admit I don't know how to write anymore but I know about feelings and if I gave vent to my feelings, it'd be the worst thing I could ever do, Shoreline Mental Health. How come everybody doesn't feel this way? Why don't the fucking moths come in? How'd I wind up spending my life sitting at typewriters? My hair hits a rabbit and it simply plays "Here comes Peter Cottontail." Otherwise I'm like Christ on the cross, I don't do anything, I don't send poems out or try to get anything published, because I'm in such a hurry to write the fucking things, I don't even type them out cleanly as they say, I never do, oh to write an aesthetic like Valery. I will I have enough work to do at this point, and no patience to last me a lifetime, little silly life that will exist for me when it's done, and I sincerely hope that when I start over to be a living being after I'm dead this time once that my small-time utopian work will not be to no avail and also that I'll never be chained to this sort of writing again (cf. Lewis and Greg's conversation about the women looking at me on the beach and not them). I tell the story of what I read in books and to your dismay use it instantly, that is this?

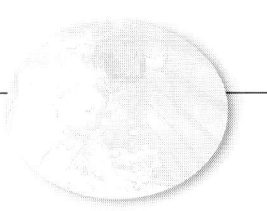

Myriad like locust or gypsy moth plague
accountability for forms and eels on toast points
like in the shoreline or borderline mental health
clinic of the bedroom community in Connecticut

you can record anything you want but you've gotta
put it in order to be generous and you don't wanna
get lost in me do you do you you glass

I can't even write a book without writing ten more
I'm not being realistic I don't know what poetry is
Or was I never take the time to stop and look

would that we really did live in that upwardly mobile
community where attention to the past was given worth
enough to last us a lifetime but none of us do

it'd be a lot easier to be a woman of letters
in such an excited state a place like that
where only a certain kind of question was asked

unfortunately this shadow train is crazy which is why
I love you so much and I can be in my mind so very old
& in the window with you fucking like a girl if I want

but when I turn upside down I get older and
I like to be reminded by the mirror that I am another
because in case you hadn't noticed the advanced timing
of this composition, in fourths it is a woman who

I'm embarrassed that breasts fall into this room
so beautifully as to be every woman's pleasure

Sweet men who were thought mean are not in the room
& many men who are and are not are watching with attention

It's exciting to feel free to be so large as communalism
or the texts on the elixir of life or the islandresses

two folds in your bookcase alarm me, it's *Robert's Rules of Order*, on a field, scarlet, the letter A gules

June 26

    Lewis and Greg just went to pick up Peggy on the 7:20 train to New Haven, Lewis has to learn the way so he can take himself to New York on Sunday for his reading. Today a pristine blue and yellow day with big white clouds, cool and even too cool to swim too much when the sun's behind a cloud. We went to Quonnipaug (did I get it right?) which surprised us for being more or less right on the road. Lewis loved the swimming there, he likes lakes. Greg didn't get wet. I keep wondering if the children drive Greg nuts but they don't seem to and he says they don't, they were doing that to me today though, there are so many emergencies and Marie and Sophia bicker so much but now Marie is singing Sophia lullabies in the hope – Marie has been a bit devious lately – that she can get Sophia to go to sleep and thus be able to wait up for Peggy to get here. I just spoke with Stephanie who had brought Sean back, we were both wondering whether both of us might not be feeding him on certain nights. She'll be here Monday, Thursday and Friday and also tomorrow, the other days she has tennis lessons. Yesterday Linda told us (no that was today) that Sean was apt to be skittish during thunderstorms but he wasn't at all yesterday; she also said he tended to get crazy once a month and rear at you (one). Today's emergency was that Sophia ate a mushroom or at least Marie said she did, it was impossible to figure out if she really had, Marie said she saw her eat it, Sophia said she didn't. I called the poison control center in New Haven and described the available mushrooms to a woman doctor who was wonderful and said the type Sophia had eaten if she had, wouldn't kill her (she didn't use those words) but would cause hallucinations and I should give her ipecac. Astonishingly, when I spoke to Maureen pretty recently, she told me the story of Kyran eating a mushroom and how we should have ipecac in the house. I went upstairs and reached sort of blindly into the medicine cabinet in the bathroom and came up with the ipecac, first thing. Sophia wouldn't take it but we managed to force her to ingest enough of it so that about 10 minutes later she did vomit. This doctor had said to look for the pieces of mushroom in her vomit, but I couldn't distinguish them from various other brown things. Sophia finally admitted that she had eaten the mushroom too and it tasted sweet. Lewis felt that we shouldn't do anything about it, he can never quite believe that there could be anything wrong, which works out in most cases. What is ipecac? Burroughs is quoted on page one of today's *Times* with a description of the ultimate cocaine high. Ipecac, a tropical South American creeping plant of the madder family, with drooping flowers. Appears between IOU and Iphigenia in the dictionary. I have great doubts about my new book, it's like making a fool of oneself again – and how distant we seem to be from the whole rest of the population of America, today on the beach some kids who were very nice to Max and gave him a balloon, made fun of the hair on my legs. Sophia came down for bread and butter. I asked her if Marie was asleep and she said, yeah but she's finding Patrick's things. This house is so wonderful and open and open, it's a great pleasure to be here and I don't mind being alone here, it's like a combination of inside and outside and very secure. Rose called today and will come up sometime next week or weekend, she's anxious for me to give her work for the magazine [*Out There*] which we've been lazy about. I've barely typed out any poems this year, even for *United Artists*, Lewis will type them on the stencils and I have no clear copies of anything, I just write them and work on them and leave them, anxious to get on to something else. I gave poems to *Mag City* and that's all. *Looking Backward* says it is impossible to understand how people could ever have lived without access to music all the time through tapes and records. This book, like all the others, gives the women short shrift (?) – though the women are described as being relieved of many of their burdensome household tasks through public services, they still aren't included in the labor force at all and all the lengthy descriptions of how work is dealt with involve only the pronoun he. So if the women don't have all this housework to do, what the hell do they do, what's your vision. It's odd that it's not even mentioned so far, it is so far from this writer's mind, I mean that one. Max fusses a lot and won't sit in the car seat, this whole life is new to him, but Lewis was saying this life made him happy in as much as it reminded him of many of our past lives in towns and countries. Here's Sophia back again, more bread and butter. She says oh look at the picture of Maxie over there, I say that's not Max that's Kyran. She says why does he have those clothes on. Suki had us talking a lot about Henniker last night and also about the Poetry Project. She and Charles B[ernstein] are trying to raise money to do a lecture series with WBAI, today Suki dropped off Maureen's colander while we were out. The beach was cold but the water was warm; sitting next to us was an extended Jewish family, one of the boys was wearing a yarmulke, and the father of the family, who had just finished being mean to his son by forcing him to swim underwater and then bragging about his achievement to all the rest of the family while the boy was weeping just as we arrived, seemed as interested in us, as a visual phenomenon, as we were in them – both of us sort of out of place in this Connecticut. We built giant swimming pools in the sand, filled them with water and then made tunnels to other pools so that the water eventually ran through three pools and back to the lake; the children enjoyed dealing with the erosion problems and water supplies and Max fell in. I've obviously written too much for today except I didn't say we had hot dogs en route with mashed potatoes and of course lettuce and this journal of this day won't include happenings after Peggy gets here. I dreamt last night I was at another Poetry Project benefit, this is my most recurrent dream! and when I woke up and remembered it, I felt I wanted to reform – what is it about the Poetry Project that takes over one's soul?!

from: Heavy Use of Cocaine Linked to Surge in Death and Illnesses [*New York Times*, June 26, 1981]

"Behind the surge in health problems appears to be a growing tendency for users of the very expensive drug to take large doses in search of what the author William Burroughs called "a rush of pure pleasure to the head."

from: *Looking Backward* [Edward Bellamy]
"It appears to me, Miss Leete," I said, "that if we could have devised an arrangement for providing everybody with music in their homes, perfect in quality, unlimited in quantity, suited to every mood, and beginning and ceasing at will, we should have considered the limit of human felicity already attained and ceased to strive for further improvements."

note: it turns out Susan said she wanted to give Steve a blowjob.

June 26

Read *Appointment at Samarra* by John O'Hara today at Lewis and Bernadette's recommendation. Felt compelled to read the whole thing today because it was one of the books Lewis took out from the library and I didn't want to prevent him from reading it, so when I opened it this morning to just check it out and found myself suddenly on page 60, prepared myself to plow all the way through and it was a perfect summer country read. When we all went into the Guilford Free Library yesterday, we didn't realize we'd be able to take out books, but by filling out cards (kind of a renegade thrill to list "poet" as occupation, Bernadette and Lewis had "writer") we all came out with some books with the prompting to finish reading them in time for bringing them back in the allotted time. Lewis was sleeping when I first started looking through the book in the kitchen this morning, the first time I've come out of the shack to go into the house and not found him out in the backyard lying on the grass overseeing the kids, reading Faulkner with half a cup of coffee next to him. Bernadette went about getting breakfast fed to the kids while I sat in the comfortable kitchen rocker, which is padded with flowered pillows, and quietly read. Even read a few pages at the lake today, which is the first time I've been able to read a book I've brought there. Usually we all just read the *Times* and some magazine or other or mostly pay attention to the children and talk when we're at the beach, Sound or today for the first time, lake. We drink beers. Today we were a little concerned that this bare-chested teenager would come over and tell us there was to be no alcoholic beverages at the beach, which was practically rule number one you see plainly on the back of the lifeguard chair as you enter, but he seemed casual and complacent enough to just lay back near behind us. A woman came around with a garbage can in her hand picking up butts amazingly enough and other stuck-up-in-the-sand pieces of wood. She didn't even look twice at us. The lifeguards and everyone who seemed to work there are all these young people. A crossing guard is provided by the town to make sure everyone gets safely across Route 77, one side of which is the parking lot and the other the town lake. There aren't many people my age, or even Lewis and Bernadette's, who seem at all interesting or even approachable. We had this discussion last night about how we actually enjoyed looking a little conspicuous and incongruous at these posh beaches. We had the messiest beach towel, Bernadette pointed out today, all covered with sand. I rubbed Bernadette's elbow as Lewis and I were leaving to go pick up Peggy at the New Haven train station, and she looks in your eyes smiling, you can't get away with that kind of stuff. I've been wanting to start a journal of this stay, especially since Bernadette started writing one as soon as we got here a week ago (she told me she said in her journal I was gregarious). So tonight as I was lying on the living room couch finishing the last pages of the novel and overhearing Peggy and her talking in the next room about Sophia (Bernadette was saying how mysterious she found her), it got me to the point where I thought I might have something interesting to report.

June 27

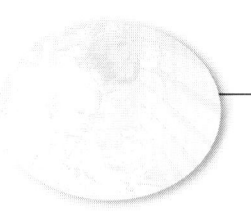

    Made complex earthworks in the sand of Quonnipaug today, six pools with interlocking canals, a castle with a moat, a self-contained mud system. Another bright and hot day, Max was blissfully hysterically happy and by the end of the day was throwing himself on all of us, Marie and Sophia like the lake better than the Sound. Lewis is upstairs working on getting his reading together, or maybe he's not, I told him to write some new poems about Connecticut so people who come to the reading will know why he's so sunburned but he said he wouldn't; I suggested collaborations. Greg has gone to the shed to read (there are two Chris's in his life) and Peggy is reading *La Methode*. Vichyssoise and barbecued chicken; Marie and Sophia have x's on their back, earthworks themselves. We saw a cardinal here in the yard and this morning a family of purple finches, many blue jays; on the road past the strawberry fields a rabbit, a lily pond and some curving thorny branches of some cultivated berry, past the raspberry plants. Collected wildflowers and ferns. We had to pay to get into the beach's parking lot today because the license number on our sticker is not the one on our car. We never have any idea of the time or even the day if it weren't for Peggy's visit and Lewis's reading. The rabbit ran like a deer. Now I want to talk to Peggy. I wish we could stay here forever, just as we are.

June 27

    Nothing happened today. Sitting on a blanket in the backyard with Bernadette and Peggy in some discussion about Marie, I said yeah, she's become a real tattletale, a goody-goody, thinking I could be straight and objective with Bernadette about her kids, like she'd respect I was being honest because I see it in her, there's no pretense about sticking up for the kids if they're rotten or something. Yesterday she asked me if I thought her and Lewis were doing the right thing in the way they didn't smack them or discipline them like storm troopers and I didn't answer much. Not having kids I have no right to say how someone should raise their kids, but now that I think about it, maybe my coming out so quick and ready saying what I did about Marie, has hurt her a little and I should bring it up next time I see her. I'd heard Lewis the day before in a father-to-daughter talk explaining to Marie what a tattle-tale was and he didn't want her reporting everything Sophia did. I was glad to hear him say that.

June 28

    Last night two skunks and a raccoon came to eat the cats' food. Lewis came downstairs to give a reading of his work about meeting the Nigerian man on 57th St. and after that we succumbed to watching the end of *The Electric Horseman*, which was awful. I thought Jane Fonda was a feminist. Dreamed about the mazes built along the walls full of sand shifting like ant colonies but for gerbils or rats. They were connected to each other by spaces with rings. Would rats and gerbils be considered gregarious? Dreamed Burroughs said he was willing to appear five days in a row at a four-day Poetry Project benefit. Then there was a vestry meeting arranged for us at Rumford St. which we kept guessing must be in Westchester. I called to complain that the people involved with St. Mark's should meet somewhere near 10th St. and 2nd Avenue, we made all sorts of plans to get there by taking a taxi from Lewis's parents' house and so on. When I woke up it took me a long while to see that Rumford St. is Russell's new address. Next a woman with a very thin waist (like in a movie) was performing with a man in a comedy. Then I was in the bathtub preparing to put on my buckskin vest (like Jane Fonda) and giving a soliloquy about Lewis. Max woke up at 6 a.m., I at 5:30, the birds were singing. Lewis left for New York at 11 with his poems. We went to an arts and crafts fair which wasn't serious, Marie and Sophia and Peggy had hotdogs, it was hot. We went to the Sound beach and met Suki, collected shells, it was low water and people were standing about with their feet in it as if at some lunatic's cocktail party, you couldn't swim at all and the water was mud, had a nice talk with Suki. At home everyone seemed to need naps – Marie, Max and Greg who finished reading *Leaving Cheyenne* first, I couldn't remember who plays Molly in the movie. The kids got grouchy and started demanding millions of things they didn't want – juice milk sandwiches, since it's Sunday there is no beer. I lose my temper, I try to mix the frozen juice in the Cuisinart, we eat dinner of pasta and salad, Lewis comes back from the city, there were a lot of people at the reading but Robin's friends and family all left after she read, everybody liked the Nigerian work and Charlotte was convinced it was a con game – that after the guy offered Lewis the wad of bills (which would be just paper) he'd find a way to go to our house and rob us, or something like that. Greg and Peggy leave for New Haven, Greg has a date and Peggy will take the train back to New York. We call Harry and Ray to wish them a happy anniversary, Ray is in her usual state of the last few months of not really communicating, Harry is considering going to see Dr. Ho, I listen to Lewis warning Ray that seeing Dr. Ho is not like going to a "regular" doctor – that there's no receptionist or waiting room! Marie, still up, eats pickles and dates. Lewis gets off the phone and turns on *American Gigolo*, really this is a glut of movies, I know I'll be tempted to watch it too like a diet of pickles and dates. I feel confused by myself, Lewis and the children, also by writing.

June 28

Driving kind of recklessly on the back roads of Guilford in some kind of defiance of there being no one awake at midnight and abandon from paying twice the usual price for beer in New Haven and there not having been much talk with Chrisi, the person I'd gone in there to see, a letdown as I keep the Jeep in fourth around the tight curves and sleepy residential streets. A New Haven cop pulled up beside me at a light and I had a beer in my hand. I just asked her how to get to the Turnpike. Two guys asked me for money while I was walking around New Haven and I wasn't the least bit compassionate answering with a swift New York no. There was a tiny kitten in the parking lot of the bar I went to in Guilford for a final beer and if it'd been there when I came out I'd have taken it home. Didn't want to pay full price for a used paperback in the 24-hour bookstore on Chapel Street after Chrisi pulled off in her VW with the flowered pillow cushion. They had three copies of *Dreaming As One*, one of Lewis' books, no Bernadette, many copies of Ted Berrigan's Corinth book, which they also had last year, a Marcuse book, some new chic book of Burroughs with namedrop pictures, no McMurtry. I would have bought any of his books for full price just having enjoyed his *Leaving Cheyenne*. This afternoon I walked into the kitchen where Bernadette and Peggy were fixing a spaghetti dinner and poured myself some Jack Daniels and joined in their conversation and eventually point to tears and say, "Look I just finished *Leaving Cheyenne*," which Bernadette has read so knows is sad. And while driving so fast on the dark streets lined with trees thinking of what Chris said last night in our hour talk on the phone about her father's hospital stuff, his having cancer, his mortality, has awoken her to a new sense of valuing life. Where she'd been suicidal, not caring one way or the other, with a series of scars on her inner forearms to prove it, now she sees the sweetness and for as long as it lasts is glad to be alive. I was just relieved she didn't mention religion – it was almost one of those revelations that might bring Christ into the conversation, and it was a relief, it was just a matter of appreciating the day to day for her. There are so many stars in the sky here in Connecticut what a pleasure to look up.

June 29

Babies let us stay in bed till quarter to eight! I've been working so hard previously tonight I can't remember anything that happened today. Maureen, when I try to type too fast on your wonderful machine, it ceases to space right, but now, as I address you it seems much better, though I think I will have to call the man. Suki called this morning around 10 to warn us that if we wanted to swim in the Sound we'd better hurry up, but we couldn't get organized fast enough, and thus went to the lake, but first (Greg didn't come, I think he'd had it with the kids, or with the beaches) we found the community center and bought another sticker; the problem with the Tintin sticker is that it so noticeably says Tintin and our license plate, in George's car, says something like 09175647, so Lewis got a new one all the while pretending to be George. The lake beach was crowded with hordes of children, you could barely swim in-between them, and women of all kinds, many pregnant women, many teachers, many camp counselors, many mothers, many young skinny girls, many beautiful women, all white women but one who was with a fascinating group of people with a 6-month-old baby whom they practically threw in the water and a boy about 2 or 3 whom they literally threw in the deep water back and forth between each other forcing the child to swim a little bit and he seemed cheerful and the baby seemed happy and not cold, I began to feel guilty that our children don't get wetter, then I began to think that this group of people was a group of professional teachers of babies to swim. There were a few young men at the beach too. We swam a lot, it got hotter, then we went to Finast to buy $36 worth of groceries, but still no leeks. (*American Gigolo* is one of the most disgusting and boring movies ever made.) Got home, Greg was on the couch, I'm not certain what book he's reading today. Unpacked the groceries and Greg went out for the beer and wine. Around dinnertime (Lewis cooked hamburgers, complaining all the while about hilarious things; we had told Greg that Quonapaug changed on June 29 into a nudist beach, with babysitting services and caves that the grownups could swim out to and make love in with free food and wine and libraries of rare editions of poetry, in fact it was a utopia, but he had missed it), Stephanie was bringing Sean back so Greg invited her to dinner and shared his hamburger with her, she ate and drank some wine and left hurriedly, but then she came back a short time later (she seemed nervous about the fact that she smelled of horse!) to hose down Sean, which was a wonderful sight, then to get the water off she used something which we all couldn't remember the name of except to call it a sweat stick, what a perfect-looking animal, she said he had been feisty today. Every child made a fuss about going to bed except Max who loves Kyran's crib I think because he sort of sinks into it and it's so comfortable and surrounded with blankets of pleasure. We could've got to work early but we got involved in some discussion of charm because Greg said he didn't like to be charming because it seemed false, so we discussed not only all the charming people we could think of but also the "old days" of the poetry world and it was just getting interesting when Greg's mother called (Maggie had called earlier) so we went to work. I was just typing out my old journal when I heard scratching at the window and turned to see a man there, quite terrified. It was just like a 19th century terror, it was Greg thinking to terrify me. I finished typing the journal, it's about 40 pages to be interspersed with the utopian information I hope and Greg came in for a beer and Lewis came downstairs for watermelon having just finished reading "impulsive" section of his book (by David Shapiro) *Neurotic Styles*. There was nothing on Home Box Office but *Urban Cowboy* so while I kept typing the rest of the notes for my book, everybody disappeared. I dreamt this morning that I was beating Peggy, it was a shocking dream to remember till I remembered that when Peggy and I were discussing our old friend Mary the other day, she had said to me that Mary was obviously of the "beat me, beat me" type, which I guess stuck in my mind. I also dreamt that I was having my fourth child (the second time I've dreamt about Ed's mother since we're here, obliquely) – what a terrifying idea, when I told Greg the dream he said oh just what you need to be completely crazy.

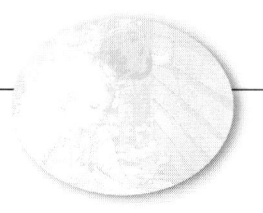

    I had some memory that Lewis had awoken in the early morning and told me he'd dreamt too that we were having another baby. Many other things happened today, and I'm not sure I am leaving out all the most important and interesting parts, I finished finally *Looking Backward* and am now reading *California's Utopian Colonies* and *Utopian Literature: A Selection,* which is a textbook with questions after each chapter. *Looking Backward* ends with the author, sorry as he is, dreaming that it is all a dream and then waking up twice, once in the 19th century and once in the 20th (in Utopia). Utopia is tutus. I must remember to look up "dirt" in the dictionary, as Marie has asked me to do. Now I must go to bed, I've worked hard today but I haven't been able to give up smoking or drinking beer yet. Each of us is getting darker every day – just the color of our skin. I'll never forget the anthroposophic doctor who told me when I was eight months pregnant to try and feel transparent.

June 29

There are clothes and toys everywhere you look in the house. Bernadette said yesterday at the beach that she's reached the point of not knowing where anything is anymore. It seems to be her who has the job of finding everything for the kids. The kids constantly are making demands. I can't see how she manages to remain relatively calm and never scream. I remove myself sometimes, like going into the living room to lay on the couch and read and inevitably fall asleep, but meanwhile I hear the kids, 'I want this I want that,' to Bernadette in the kitchen and the most excited she'll get is to just say, 'go away.' In her voice is the quiver that says in another minute I'm going to be a total helpless lunatic, but she puts up with it. Driving Peggy back to New Haven last night I said, wanting to talk about Bernadette, who she's been best friends with since grade school, "She's so great." Bernadette looked at me with a little smile earlier when she asked if I'll be coming home tonight, since I'm going to see a friend in New Haven after I drop Peggy off. "Yeh, probably," I say in a way which sums up for her the state of that affair. And I'm saying something I'd been thinking about and by trying to express it to Peggy find the idea, which is that it amazes me that she, Bernadette, or any person with an ego as big as a writer's, can submit to the humiliation of catering to these little pipsqueaks. All of Bernadette's talk of Utopias and here she's faced with three nagging kids constantly asking for juice or where's my other sneaker. We've all made references to wishes that we had a servant, someone to do the shopping and to take care of the children while we read and write all day. I make my token attempts at helping, picking screaming Max up from between Bernadette's legs as she's preparing the thousandth peanut butter or cream cheese and jelly sandwich on white bread. I take him to the living room couch and put on the *5th Brandenburg Concerto*. Then the *6th* follows and that sounds more like it with half-step movement in the bass riding so beautiful. Remarkably Max lays peacefully in there and I can start reading an Erich Fromm book while Marie comes in and distracts me continuing doing the girly kind of dancing she'd begun in the kitchen while I was sitting there making rhythms on a straw rattle. She actually made some pretty graceful ballet kind of moves making me miss Cynthia more and wishing she'd come up quick. Her address isn't in Bernadette's address book. The only crisis up here in the country is that I can't find a nail clipper and that twice in a row we've run out of beer on Sunday when none of the stores are allowed to sell it, which is just as repressive as the articles on book banning I've been reading in various papers lately making me afraid of what this new administration is bringing about. There is the constant sounds of birds from out the window, layers of different calls, and the breeze through the bushes. A fly on the screen, the unprintable thoughts in my printing press brain.

June 30

Tuesday though we've lost track again of the days. I slept late this morning, after waking Lewis got up with the children, I read a chapter of *California's Utopian Colonies* (Lewis is reading so many books simultaneously I can't even find out what they all are to list them; I'll add a list as addendum A to this journal), then falling back to sleep with pleasure and dreaming I am in a museum at an opening of a show of famous old paintings, I suddenly notice and turn to Lewis to tell him that all the people who are walking through the gallery are the same people as the people in the paintings, and, I say to Lewis, including you! I realize that Lewis is a man in one of my favorite paintings, a painting of some "Gentleman from Verona" or something like that in the Metropolitan Museum, and that painting also resembles (oh god I can't say this) that actor in *American Gigolo*!, so, they are serving petit fours but when you eat one the wind in the museum is so furious as to whip the chocolate frosting into swirls in the air. We couldn't get too organized and by the time we did it got cloudy but we set out to go to the beach anyway, we stopped to get some pictures of mine all taken in New York of the Poetry Project and the inside of the church and of the children, the best ones are one of Sophia lounging in a chair at her grandparents' house and one of the backyard of the church, one of the interior, looking clean as a new art gallery with ladders and pristine clear windows and one of the office with Gary reflected in a mirror. Rose just called and said she'd be up in two hours, Grace is also coming tonight to meet her long-lost god-daughter from the Ozarks so they can proceed to go by New London Ferry to camp at Montauk Point with the rest of their family. Spoke to Maggie today and she and Cynthia have a great desire to be here and might come up for a day over the weekend, also Maggie has to bring the NYSCA contracts which need my signature, something has to be done for a revised budget for the NEA within ten days, which seems precipitous. I mean what if I had gone to Antarctica for a vacation, as well I might have if I could afford it and if I didn't have so many children, but anyway also at the drugstore Greg had to get a nail clipper and then he clipped all the children's nails while we were waiting for Lewis to emerge from the library where he returned *Leaving Cheyenne* and *Appointment in Samarra* so we could get two more books (they'd only let us take out two each for a week till we got real cards) and they said they'd called Maureen, our reference and she was away, so we had to give another reference so we mentioned Suki but Lewis didn't know her address so he ran out to the car to get it and then came back with *As I Lay Dying* and *Butterfield 8*, H.G. Wells' *A Modern Utopia*, another Utopian anthology and something else. We tried to stop at two different opticians to get Lewis's glasses fixed so that the lens doesn't so frequently fall out of the frame, but they were either closed or out to lunch. We toyed with the idea of having pizza which, when we decided not to, upset Sophia tremendously, as you can never proffer the possibility of food to her without coming through. We went to the Sound but just to the playground, it was cold and windy. I think we were talking about Faulkner and then we came home. I have a note here to myself to mention heresies and exercises, I am most confused about my writing and what I wanted to say was I was glad there were so many copies of issues of *Heresies* here because I needed them for what I'm writing and then I was going to go into what my exercise routine is, six salutes to the sun, a number of bending and curving at the waist exercises followed by the ostrich, then the lotus position – head to the ground – hands behind back exercise followed by some dancing, then the lion and the loosening of the neck one, then some of Lewis's new back exercises from Dr. Ho, then shoulder stands and the plough, followed by rest, then some athletic feats like standing upside down on hands and knees and walking on knees if I feel like it, all done as slowly as possible. We had a weird dinner tonight of chicken noodles and peas, it was like an old dinner your old grandmother might've fixed, I was in a bad mood and I had just gotten my period for just the third time now after two years without it, read a long article in *Signs* about menopause to see if there was something I could tell Hannah [Weiner] but it was really too erudite for words. Yesterday Hannah sent two Holly Hobbie notebooks for the children and we got a postcard from Bob Holman in San Diego, went and scared Greg in the shed, yet we didn't scare him as much as he scared me last night. At dinner we seem to usually talk about books and children, as much as the children will let us talk. Max is being very demanding, I'm not looking forward, nor is Lewis, to this next year, when Max is between 1-1/2 and 2-1/2 years-old, though he goes to sleep happily and readily still. Though he can't be nursing very much when he pretends to if I get my period now precisely every 28 days. The sun came out later today, it never did rain, and it was just as nicely hot as ever. Now soon Grace and then Rose will appear.

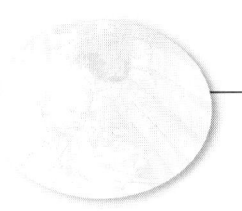

Note: Poetry Project will officially get (if all goes well with NEA): $21,000 from NYSCA and $29,200 from NEA, plus I learned today it seems likely that some money will come from the Kaplan Fund but definitely not from Lucius or Eva Eastman or Metropolitan Life.

June 30

Had to stop writing letter to Michael to get to journal as I feel myself getting tired and wanting to get back to Alaska in the book I'm reading, *Coming Into the Country*, which is as fine writing as seems possible. Another day of nothing spectacular. There is a skunk or a few skunks who have been coming around eating out of the cats' dish in the yard. We all gather at the door to watch and in one of those observances Bernadette tried to get up close, scared it off and I was glad it didn't spray though we smelt spray the other night which was given off for no apparent reason. There was also a raccoon reported by Bernadette but no one else saw it. I felt brave enough to let Sean, the horse, nuzzle me under the armpit. It seems as if he wanted to be able to lift me up with his nose, but I sensed he was just being affectionate so my continuous attempt to communicate with him on a friendly level may be advancing. A bunch of visitors came up tonight and though for a while it was nice I wanted to get back out here to finish my letter and work and read. Eventually I tore myself away, which was a feat since Rose is in there now laying on the floor with no shirt on watching *Electric Horseman* on HBO (which we watched the other night), I guess it's her country apparel. She brought a friend, Denise. Also, Grace is up waiting for her cousin who she hasn't seen in 10 years to come meet her here so they can take off for a trip. Grace had presented the thrill of the day previous to that view of Rose by showing us the scars on her knees from having had them broken in a bad car wreck. In the afternoon, it ended up being too cold to stay on the beach but we went anyway to Jacob's Beach for the kids since there's a playground there that they like. They run from one ride to another – from swing set to this four-seater horse whirl thing to another set of littler kid swings to the sliding pond. It was hot when we started to get ready to go to the beach – Bernadette preparing sandwiches, getting the towels together, the kids putting on their bathing suits – but as we were getting in the car the sky was clouding up and I didn't bother to put on shorts since it was cool too, but having gone so far we just continued as routine. Lewis wanted to get his glasses fixed, but the first place was closed and the second place was closed for lunch. So with Sophie demanding pizza we headed over to the beach. Before that we'd stopped at the library to return the books we've finished. Since Marie and Sophie didn't have shoes – Bernadette said, Marie I sent you out to check that your shoes were in the car and you said yes (Marie seems to be lying a lot lately, she also told me she'd locked the gate which separates Sean's shed from the neighbor's, but when I checked later it wasn't) – only Lewis could go in. He came out with six books – another John O'Hara book for me, *Butterfield 8*, which he says is much better than the one we've both just read, a Utopia book for Bernadette who's reading lots of them now in preparation and research for a project she's at work on, *Sound and The Fury* and *Light in August* in one volume which he wants me to read, and collected poems of Thomas Hardy. I think that's all of them. They didn't have a copy of *Terms of Endearment*, which is the only book I would have taken out until I finish the McPhee. Once we got to the playground we tried to read the *Times* in the strong wind, which wasn't too successful. Once when the wind blew the paper Bernadette was holding into Lewis' face he accused her of hitting him and bopped her on the head with the section he'd been reading kind of playfully, but how playful are those gestures. Everyone was sitting in the grass reading the newspaper while the kids went back and forth between us and the rides, under the big sky with the Sound right over there if you'd look stretching might as well be the ocean except you can barely discern Long Island on the horizon. Chris calls late from Manhattan. We've been having these long talks at night while she's been staying at her parents' house taking care of her mother while her father is in the hospital. Last week they discovered cancer. Today they gave him a year to live. I'm surprised that I feel genuine emotion for someone I don't know. I can't help having the selfish sense of knowing that the year or so coming will make it difficult for me and Chris, as well as for her and her family, as she will need to be there a lot since she's so close to them, meaning she won't be with me. I think she's a little drunk as she's talking to me since she's repeating things, I let her, and keeps telling me she misses me. I want to get her to cry, to be able to get it off herself, but it's so long distance the idea seems ludicrous. I can only say I feel bad for her and say wish we were together so that she could cry and I want to hold her. But up here everything back in New York, my whole life, all the connections, seem so far away and it's almost straining to say I miss you.

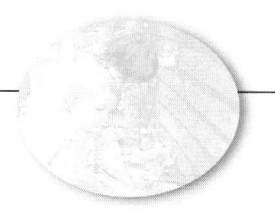

July 1

Max woke up this morning and stood in his crib for perhaps an hour, silent. I looked out the window and saw Rose doing T'ai chi ch'uan, Lewis dreamt he was driving a taxi in the Bronx, Grace woke up giggling. Rose and Denise made a mushroom omelet then Grace made farmer's omelets with mushroom. Rose, Denise and Greg went to the lake first and we all followed, there were millions of people there, it was hot and cloudy, Rose swam back and forth along the floats for hours, we built pools and canals quickly, Sophia stepped on them, Rose and Denise left to look at the Sound, we came home and Grace made zuppa di pesce, Stephanie and Suki came by, Stephanie took Marie for a ride on Sean, Suki left a copy of her grant proposal with Charles and *Memories of a Hostess*, Rose and Denise went back to New York, we supped, it rained, Greg sprayed Marie and Sophia with the hose, we put the children to bed, I doctored Grace's foot. I cannot seem to "think" about poetry. Last night Grace told all about the time she "died." Rose wore two bathing suits, the fish store only has expensive fish, the canals, Sophia goes in deep, we also all ate cantaloupe, plums, bananas, watermelon, blueberries, tomatoes and apples. Sophia and Marie pushed the screen out of their window and shouted, Rose is stealing all the lettuce! No mail, Max peed and shat on the floor. We went down a beautiful road called Three Mile Course, there are no more strawberries to be had from the fields. Grace says maybe something really momentous is going on in the world, last night we sneaked up on the shed and scared the wits out of Greg, except he wasn't scared. We tried to go to see if Sean was sleeping lying down late at night but he was awake and a little frenzied, saw another skunk then too. I'm sorry I can't think of anything more to tell, or anything that sounds more interesting than this stuff (Sophia thought a tractor was a cow) but it was a day that went on its own bringing us along slightly exhausted, to meet its kind of spirit which was not bland at all not dangerous not carelessly put together. There was an old man or woman swimming very slowly through the middle of the lake, silent also for a long time.

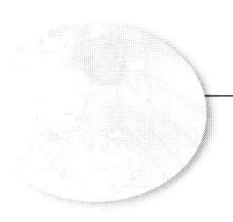

July 1

    Was basically quiet not knowing what to say with Rose and her friend from Chicago who came up last night and left around 4 this afternoon to go back. "I just couldn't take the city," says Rose, who wanted to swim her laps in unchlorinated water. Apparently, she does laps everyday, and for 45 minutes this morning I'm a little startled that someone has the strength or stamina to actually keep swimming for that length of time. "Laps, boring," she says. While she's out there at the far boundary swimming parallel to the buoys, Denise and I are together on a blanket, her mostly lying out getting, for lack of anything else to do, a tan, while I sit mostly reading about Alaska not making much of an attempt at communicating since she's not either. I find out she's a bartender at a gay bar in Chicago. She says it will be changing its name to go along with its new open door policy. "Gay women don't go out much, don't go to the bars like gay men." After asking her what section of Chicago she lives in, I feel like I must sound pretty boorish to have asked those typical questions. Her smiles are friendly and I'm tempted to rub her back and ass as she's layed out in her tight bathing suit and fantasize good things. I think everybody's content enough to be not talking much but just relaxing at a beach under the sun. The second carload meets us after a while – Bernadette and Lewis, kids and Grace – and eventually I get caught up in a canal and pool system we're digging in the sand. Bernadette and I have done most of the digging. I'm oblivious to the other children who come over to gaze and admire our work, I don't even look up, and don't let Max take the shovel I'm using though it's his. He's so easily distracted that in another fraction of a second he's involved with some other activity, i.e., taking the pail, turning it over, smacking it a few times on the top, then turning it back over, voila. What are you doing?, Grace asked from the living room as I was going through the drawers in Maureen's study looking for an envelope. Her and Bernadette are talking and giggling. Bernadette is layed out in the bean bag chair, a few empty Rolling Rock bottles next to her. It's a cozy conversation looks like and I don't feel like getting involved, don't sense an invitation to join in and that's ok. Getting a letter together, I say, and find a pen to write Michael's name and address and my return address remembering the Guilford ZIP code, and without even a side trip to the refrigerator leave the house making sure the screen door doesn't slam behind me. While I'm outside I decide to get the nail clippers I've left in the car. Reaching around in the dark for them and recognizing the sandiness of the seats from everyone getting in the car after the beach and recognizing Max's car seat strapped in the middle of the back seat, I realize I have fond feelings for this car. Crawling around in it as it sits in the driveway at dark, it's like returning to somewhere you've lived a long time but have been away from for awhile. In the stillness, I remember the way it usually is, with Bernadette seated in the space I'm reaching across holding Max who has been squirming to get out of the car seat. She's probably just pulled a breast out of her loose bathing suit to nurse him. Lewis would be driving, his right hand delicately wiping fallen strands of hair out of his eyes, wrapping them around his right ear. Depending on his mood he's either singing silly word songs to Sophie buckled into the seatbelt right next to him or taking account of what provisions are necessary, asking Bernadette what we need. Lewis has exactly the same car radio habits as me, changing stations a lot when it seems possible to find a decent song, settling for middle of the road crap (putting up with it to have something when it's necessary to compromise all your principles and taste), and leaving it off when you forget about it or just want the quiet. The one time I disagreed with his selection and was about to reach over and change the station, something I wondered whether I had the right to do, in that ethical second he reached over and changed it. The car belongs to George Schneeman who leaves it parked up here for when his family goes up to Maine. The insurance runs out I think tomorrow, but I don't think I'll bring that up. George has given us permission to use the car and for the six of us driving to the beaches, it is certainly more comfortable than Maureen's Jeep. I then feel my way in the dark to the mail box and put my letter in for the mailman to pick up tomorrow morning. Back inside sitting back down at my typewriter I hear a funny rustling sound. Turning off the humming typewriter I realize it's just started pouring rain. Now to cut my toenails and go back to Alaska.

[Bernadette page unreadable (bad Xerox)]

July 2

Grace says that my remorse for having gotten excited and yelled at her is peculiar. We were talking about the time the two of us were driving a truck with Lewis and Bernadette's stuff – in their move from Henniker, N.H. to NYC – and as we came off the 59th Street

Bridge, Grace had made too sharp a turn and gotten us stuck for a moment in an overpass. We're sitting in the kitchen eating bowls of ice cream recalling our police run-ins, brought on because I mention I've already had some ice cream today, as if it's a sin to eat it twice in one day. I bring up my arrest at a Friendly's when I was 16 (the cat sitting in my lap just typed three letters). From there Grace brings up the times we've helped Bernadette and Lewis move, which we always seem to bring up when we see each other. Driving the 36-foot truck down from Henniker we stopped for breakfast at a diner. A few other trucks were parked there. On entering we felt like all the other truck drivers. Polished aluminum behind the counter, stools at the long counter with a few morning stragglers and regulars finishing up some coffee. One trucker is lingering one extra moment in front of his plate smeared with a little catsup left over from his scrambled eggs. Juke boxes at each booth. We take a seat and are immediately brought two tall glasses of cold, clear ice water. It's so perfect and swallowed so quickly I have to ask for another when the waitress comes back to take our order. At twilight tonight the sky seemed like it'd be clear enough to look at stars using the star book Grace has brought up (by H.A. Rey, the same guy who along with the woman to whom he was married, Margret, wrote *Curious George*). We both peer out the back screen door, Grace pointing at the horizon where there are purple and dark orange streaks of cloud indicating that the rest of the sky is clear. Twenty minutes later, after we look through the book a little bit and figure out how to align the chart, we walk outside and it's clouded up so much we can't see any stars. So we walk around to the side of the house to poke our faces in at Bernadette's window where she's typing single space, but don't scare her with our ghost sounds as everyone's been alerted to this game since I really did scare her the other day. That time, when she turned to the window and saw my face, she experienced real shock. I saw her so vulnerable it was like a privilege, but then I regretted giving her a scare though we both were laughing kind of, but then I didn't know what to do or say. It was an awkward moment. The space between thoughts. A gypsy moth fell on me while we were sitting on the grass so blissfully drinking coffee and wine tonight. It was obviously dying since it wouldn't fly off as I poked it and finally had to flick it off. As I did that I noticed its body still resembled its pre-metamorphisized state of caterpillar. Do moths remember what it was like being a caterpillar, totally defoliating most of New England, 1981? Cynthia just called to announce her and Maggie's arriving time tomorrow. Bernadette, on the extension, sounds a little down. Once Cynthia hangs up she and I continue talking via phone. She's down because her work isn't going so well. I say I'm just writing journal stuff, which is fun and which can get ambitious, but starts anyway as fun. The phone is signaling us to get off with "please hang ups" and a loud busy signal, so regrettably we do finally have to get off, both back to work.

July 3

It's, uh, eve of the fourth of July, airplanes are flying over Guilford and firecrackers are modestly going off, two skunks came to eat the cat food and fought, gurgled and sprayed. Maggie and Cynthia arrived this afternoon while we were at the beach, the lake beach, where, the moment we arrived, it began to rain. Greg was dressed all in white when he went to pick them up. So we all drove back here, respectively, amidst the torrent and sat, talked, Sophia would not stop talking about this ghost Maureen told us about and I made the mistake of telling Marie about, even to the extent of its one leg, so then Sophia wouldn't go upstairs at all alone. Lewis and Maggie are asking me, "When did David come?" Cynthia and Greg are outside, perhaps looking for stars. This morning Sophia put butter on the floor because I wouldn't give her food fast enough, Max dumped lemonade all around and chipped a plate and Lewis got mad at me for getting angry at the children. Then I gave Marie a plate of eggs to bring upstairs to Lewis and she left it in the bedroom, he never found it. Dark clouds all over the place. Grace left this morning to meet her long-lost cousin from the Ozarks at the New London ferry to go over to Montauk Point. *Life in the Iron Mills*. The rain was warm and beautiful but all the people, including the children, are so distracting from what? Lewis has decided to stay downstairs tonight, which is shocking, and talk. Marie's still awake. We had pasta for two million, somebody's playing the piano. I feel like I am following a script but I'd best not start talking about any of that because sentences that begin "I feel like" don't exactly have any real ending. I am confused within the second statue of country life and the 100th stage of family. I wish Grace were still here. Marie's going to bed, Greg put a match, no, I can't say that. *California's Utopian Colonies* is a depressing book, it's nearly done. Not only that I can't continue writing at all because I keep listening to this conversation about St. Mark's in the next room, which maybe if I take part in it wholeheartedly, will free me from all my Poetry Project dreams. What a mess! Today doesn't seem to have made any sense at all, maybe later tonight could, yet who would wonder or I cannot complete a sentence I cannot.

July 3

Yesterday when we went to the beach the weather was so weird there were only a few other people. The wind was very strong blowing in off the Sound and it seemed like the highest and roughest the tide could get, except for a storm talked about around here for years. The waves were choppy and there were a lot of whitecaps, but the temperature was ok. Sitting on the beach, with it not crowded for a change, was actually pretty adventurous besides feeling peaceful. A few yards away from us were two older ladies who had their backs to the ocean. That seemed rude. The lifeguard, wrapped in a towel, probably thinking about what else she could be doing, just stared out to sea and didn't turn her head to look over at us who were a short distance away. We stayed as long as possible savoring the privacy, chatting, me twirling the kids around for awhile, grateful we had such a powerful open view to ourselves. There wasn't even anybody checking passes as we drove into the lot.

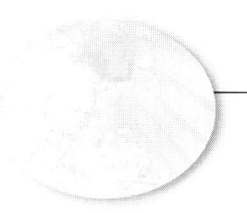

    Driving the Jeep on the horrible Connecticut Turnpike with banshee trailer trucks whooshing by on each side headed into New Haven to go pick up Cynthia and Maggie who've come to visit for how many days. I got stuck in an amazing downpour which resulted in a four or five car collision I eventually passed after being stuck in the backed up traffic. I had to drive in first gear heading up the grade onto the bridge over the Quinnipag River right outside the city. I had my foot on the truck-like clutch in the stop-and-go traffic worrying about how late I'm going to be and wondering whether they would have the sense to be waiting or might they head into town. The fragile Jeep, especially on the Turnpike, feels as safe as driving aluminum foil. The windshield wipers weren't exactly working. I had to summon control as I wondered what being crazy is about, the wipers screeching obnoxiously. And the toll booth collector totally ignored my pleasant hello. So everyone's presumably still sitting on blankets in the backyard now, because the weather here is so transient that now the sun is out. I had to get away from Sophia who is repeating everything till someone acknowledges her and will disappear for a second only to come back with a new set of messages or bring back an old favorite and refuses to go away. I wanted to write about yesterday's wind and the trip to New Haven anyway. Sorry Bernadette for complaining. Cynthia and Maggie had great welcoming smiles as I drove by the railroad station waving before making the turn to load them in. Bernadette greeted them with "Welcome to our Utopia." We never made it away from the dining room table after dinner. I cleared away the dishes and got them rinsed and in the dishwasher, which has been my main function since Bernadette and whoever's been visiting prepare the meals. We're all talking till we ended the night moved somehow into the kitchen where I heated up saki and served everyone at least two cups. The first few hours we were talking mostly about dance and poetry, the Judson Theater, how there's never a big audience for new work, what all those dancers involved then are up to now – some dead, some wasted – scenes, Naropa Poetry Wars, click jealousies, how dance is more entertaining than poetry, etc. It was so much more interesting than the subsequent next hour's talk about administrative problems at St. Mark's, but we all stayed in the room, no one willing to leave, for the first time none of the three housesitters going off to work, though Bernadette excused herself for awhile to write in her journal which we heard being typed in the room next to where we sat continuing our conversation. A giant moth, sort of a behemoth, fascinated the dinner party at one point. It had orange and black markings on a section of its wings but the markings would disappear as the wings were folded in. After everyone went upstairs to bed, I sat in the kitchen rocker and had one more cup of saki. I had my arm halfway to my lips for at least five minutes just sitting still, then became conscious of the position I was in and held it for another minute or two imagining I was being filmed. No one came down.

July 4

    July 4 it rains all day, it rains sometimes in torrents, often lightly continuously, we spent a lot of time outside getting wet. Stacy came over to play, the other day I had to go into her house to retrieve Marie and Sophia who Stacy's mother pronounced well-behaved children, they were impressed with Stacy's traditional little-girl room, like something in a TV show. We played in the mud, Cynthia and Maggie danced, poured the cold bitter water from the pump all over ourselves, children fell in the mud. I made some food, we went to the Sound beach anyway, stood in the rain and watched the various jellyfish, no one swam, we collected shells and got wet and sandy, there was one other crazy family on the beach like us, the dark clouds were changeable, occasional spare firecrackers went off, we found mussels nursing at seaweed. Lewis and Greg had watched the tennis match, that guy McEnroe won. A couple of days ago Linda told me that Calamity Jane's letters to her daughter were a fraud. Last night there was a most wonderful moth in the room, a large lepidopterous thing whose wings looked like a brown embroidered cloak but when the wings opened unusually wide, there was a "dress" of orange and purple designs beneath. It rested on my hair for a while. The skunks were fighting over the cat food then too, they make a gurgling noise. My dream is completely forgotten, we made love very quietly. We had all been talking about dance and poetry, and some about St. Mark's of course. Maggie tells me that David feels Anne [Waldman]'s being in town will create some "competition" between me and her! He is so weirdly uninformed. Though he wants her to do fund-raising for the Projects [Poetry Project, Danspace] with Yoko Ono, and has been talking about it for six months, he has not mentioned it to Anne yet. At midnight Greg heated some saki for us. After the beach Lewis made hamburgers and hot dogs which we ate with the coleslaw and potato salad I'd made earlier and beans, sauerkraut and ice cream, this meal our donation to America. Clark [Coolidge]'s two books came yesterday, plus letters from Bill Corbett. I wrote to Summer and to Jeanne Lance about the Ear Inn reading. I can't imagine what I'll have to read at it, I can't write poetry anymore, I can't even think it, as I said before, except for the titles: Shoreline Mental Health and Eels On Toast Points, and even they have their deficiencies as titles. The thing that obsesses me most is not poetry but the uses of the Cuisinart, and also guilt about still smoking. Grace said it's best not to be perfect because how would you feel then. Maggie is reading *The Well of Loneliness* and Cynthia *Appointment in Samarra*. I think Lewis is reading the Mayakovsky book and I'm beginning H.G. Wells's *A Modern Utopia*. I think Greg is still reading John McPhee. The children are all asleep and it's still light out. Linda told me that the brown gypsy moths which are everywhere are males and the white ones, which are the ones I'm used to thinking of as gypsy moths, are females – there are fewer than two females in our little environs which seems to mean that the spray is more threatening to the "weaker sex." Sean kissed me today. We played ball, Sophia was able to catch the deflated basketball for the first time, we cheered her after each catch and when we did she fell to the ground and hid her head behind the ball laughing. Like a saint, I keep thinking that everyone is so much "better" than me. I realized that the dream about NELLIE (these capitals are always an error) was really about Greg of course and what it was about was learning in what ways he's different, knowing him living together, than I'd always assumed he was before. I've been keeping journals since I was 17 years old, even before that, but now they are becoming more and more difficult – I cannot for the life of me remember what has happened! And the formations of the sentences seem more and more arbitrary and strange, inconsequent to the events and other stuff, especially feelings and impressions most of which you can't say anyway unless you're writing to no one, which is the best way, but in this case I'm not, which is a funny discipline. I am certainly in a quandary about all writing as a result of my time done at Poetry Project. Later I will check for skunks again.

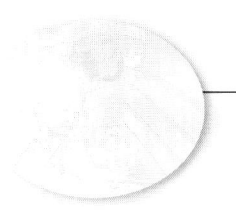

July 4

As Lewis was filling up the bottles for Marie and Sophie, he asked me if I'd finished reading my book yet. I had gotten this bedtime process started by taking the juice out of the freezer knowing he'd be coming down after reading a book or two to the kids. I was finishing off cleaning the dishes with Maggie, Cynthia was curled up on the living room couch napping, Bernadette was getting Max into bed. I said no, my rhythm had been interrupted by having guests these last days. After dinner we'd all ended up outside playing ball. Lewis and I threw this sponge football back and forth across the yard for a good long time. We agreed we should do it every day. It was drizzling lightly but we've been out all day under the gray skies and occasional light rain. When the ball hit a tree, the person catching would get a little sprinkling. We all then wound up watching Bernadette and Sophia play catch with a deflated basketball, Bernadette lobbing the ball into Sophia's outstretched arms. When she'd catch it we'd all cheer and applaud, even Max imitating us. She'd crumble to the ground on top of the ball laughing and giggling. In the afternoon, sitting on the couch with Cynthia, she asked me how am I finding the kids. I said fine, Marie's no problem and Sophia's mysterious raw nature dazzles me even if at times annoys me. I have to respect her aggressive uncontained energy. Walking into the house after our romp after dinner I said to Lewis, yeh that was great, as I was hoping the dishes would be done. But alas, Cynthia had gone to sleep and Maggie was left reading a Superman comic. Maggie, Cynthia and I were singing all the old songs we could remember as Bernadette typed in the next room. Chapel of Love, Wandering Man, It's My Party and I'll Cry if I Want To (Lesley Gore went to Cynthia's school, Sarah Lawrence, and would be dropped off and picked up by a limo), Judy's Turn to Cry, Soldier Boy, He's So Fine, 100 Pounds of Clay. We couldn't remember the verse. One song that Bernadette called out we'd never heard, 10 Commandments of Love. Eventually we turned on the TV because *Woodstock* was on and when Bernadette and later Lewis came down we ended up watching the end of that. Then the ridiculous news came on. Because it's July 4th, it aired these purportedly patriotic segments, but seemed to me condescending in highlighting ethnic groups by showing boat people, hot dog vendors and garment district guys wheeling racks through midtown. Though we were drinking piña coladas through all of this, it was like the typical "locked into the tube not talking to each other" syndrome and I was for smashing the TV and singing more songs.

July 5

Max woke up too early, refused to sit in the high chair, fussed for about four hours after which I fell asleep outside in the rain wrapped in Marie's blanket. I went upstairs to take a real nap and while Greg was disc-jockeying in the living room my dreams were orchestrated by the music he was playing which began with "The fly has married the bumble bee" and ended somewhere around Philip Glass. I dreamed Lewis and the kids and I were being chased down a road like the Dempster Highway through the Arctic by men with machine-gun rifles, I think they shot a stream of water, we got out of our car near our house, which was a dangerous place to be, and I suggested we take the first bus that pulled up to nowhere (utopia), Lewis didn't like the idea. In a very orange dream I was cutting Grace's hair and Maggie's and teaching Marie how to cut her nails (seashells) while Stacy's mother and another suburban woman were trying to induce me to go to a dinner theater. Like the children, they were actually pushing in the bathroom door to get to me (Bill Berkson's question about whether haircuts, getting them, is sexy). Greg and I were lying on the beanbag chair watching TV and I noticed he is a hermaphrodite (like putting Sophia's bathing suit on Max? it's pink and shiny). When I woke up the sun came out, we started to go to the beach, it went in again, we played baseball, it came out again, we went to the lake and finally swam. Maggie, Cynthia and I are each having such completely differing shapes, hair and colors. We ate dinner at the lobster place where the corn is roasted black with part of the husk and you get all sooty eating it and you get to handle the lobster and the clams eating outdoors behind the big smoky fire, you feel like an enraged gentle cannibal, make a big mess of the table, dinner for 8, $35 without the tip, the waitress's name was Carrie. Home we put the children to bed pretty easily, Max can do so much talking all of a sudden, can say bye bye and ball and door, tries to say horse but can't do it, but he can talk about the horse, I imitate his imitation sentences for Marie and Sophia and they ask me to do it again and again, it seems like a lot of the time he is saying something like: seems mama like a lot of ha ha ha, if you whisper in his ear, door door, he will laugh crazily. Maggie showed me the NYSCA and NEA contracts and we went over the revised budgets and then Greg drove her and Cynthia to New Haven for the train. Maggie lost her wallet, Greg his notebook. Lewis is reading Rimbaud, he said Rimbaud's poems that he wrote at 10 and 11 years old are great. I said how did he get to write poems at that age, Lewis said because he was a rebel. Greg is watching TV. Last night Greg invited Cynthia to go for a walk in the rain, but she didn't. Tonight the skunks are back, the cats came into the house, and the most enormous raccoon is outside now foraging among the cat food. The two younger cats hiss at each other and don't really get along. I answered all of Bill's questions last night, now the phone rings, it's Peggy, we talk about New York, country and all friends. Now I go to make more notes on utopian books (I realized today that I want only to read the books about imaginary utopias, which is the real meaning of the word, and not study any more communes or socialist propagandas), write a note to Hannah thanking her for the Holly Hobbie notebooks (the same kind she writes her short poems in) that she sent for the children, and write the covering letter for the interview of Bill. Then if I had my way I'd stay up for as many hours as I could keep my eyes open reading, but instead I'll go to sleep lying face down on Maureen and Ted's most comfortable bed, thinking about playing softball and sex.

July 5

In a little while I have to drive Maggie and Cynthia back to New Haven so they can get the train back into New York. Last night I asked Cynthia, as it looked like things were winding down, if she wanted to take a walk in the rain. She said I'd rather not or something like that (she'd taken her pants and shirt off right after dusk and gone into the backyard to get wet from the rain that'd been falling on and off all day). I had one of the cats in here with me last night for a while but it was being too affectionate as I was trying to go to sleep so I had to throw him out. The day took a long time before anything got going as a group. At one point I was playing a lot of albums, one or two cuts from each one, eventually feeling like a WBAI disc jockey – Maureen's Irish records, early Donovan (I remembered most of the lyrics), Philip Glass, Judy Collins, Randy Newman and Edwin Denby's poem on *The World Record*. No one was bothering me as I mostly stood there listening – Bob Dylan borrowed, stole, appropriated the tune and some phrases for his early song, "Bob Dylan's Dream" ("As I was on a train going west") from the Irish traditional song "Lord Franklin." Bernadette, coming down from upstairs where she'd been napping, said I'd orchestrated her dreams since you can hear any sound from one part of the house in any other. Her hair was parted on the side instead of the usual middle. Lewis asked me if I found Marie, who was running around with no pants on, sexy. I said yeh. I like the way the wooden stairs creak whenever someone's on them. It announces their approach. In the kitchen the sound of Lewis' typewriter in the room directly above only a wood plank away is like gunfire. This afternoon as I was reading *The Tale of Peter Rabbit* to Marie, she corrected my pronunciation of the word "sieve," matter of factly but with assuredness. I just said alright and kept reading.

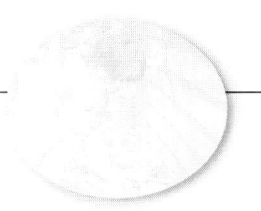

July 6

We got mail today but there wasn't anything for us but I got a letter from Peggy in which she told me all the things we'd talked about on the phone the other night but she didn't tell me then she'd written a letter. Max is getting more and more insistent when he wakes up. I slept late this morning after reading H.G. Wells for a while, it was finally sunny out and very hot, Marie and Sophia had gone over to play with Stacy, we began to organize our trip to the beach and when I went to get them they were sitting outside at a little children's table with little children's cups and plates and knives and forks having peanut butter and jelly sandwiches on white bread with milk in little tiny children's plastic cups, but the main thing was they had on incredible costumes and giant hats, all sorts of festooned haberdashery and Sophia kept shouting "this is my disco dress, see see!" and for some reason all this made me mad however I didn't let on, then Rex and Jane?, Stacy's parents, invited me in again and I had to talk to them about where we come from and who we are and about how fat Max is compared to Kyran, or how fat they were as babies, and they sort of apologized for feeding the kids without asking me and I said that's o.k. as long as they don't have sweets and then they said well would it be ok to give them one marshmallow, because when I got there the kids had been shouting to me, now we're going to have dessert! So, passive person that I am, I said ok one marshmallow and then I told them to come home after they were finished, poor Stacy it turns out punched Sophia and poor my children after she did they had to witness her being "spanked"! I hate other people! So forgive me, anyway,

I finally got my children back after this cultural trauma during which I was self-conscious about my hairy legs and low-cut bathing suit (& I do believe Sophia must've hit Stacy too) (& Stacy's parents – the Schnooks? that's what the kids say is their last name) invited us to come and swim in their pool but I can't understand why they would have a pool when the beaches, all three of them of such variety as to suit any taste in swimming, are only an inch away) anyway by the time I got back to the house (& then I found out they'd given the kids Kool-Aid after telling me they didn't give their child sugar, now I'm beginning to think I'm all wrong about sugar, after all it's not maple syrup I'm against or homemade ice cream either, and now Greg has pointed out to me that these are just impressions of Stacy's parents, having perhaps nothing to do with the truth and what do I expect of them? (he's reading Rousseau)) but when I did get back to the house Barbara and Chassler had called and they were on their way here, they'd been staying in a motel in Branford where there is a funny thing in the bathroom that turns into a sort of steambath and when they came they were with Nan, an old friend of Barbara's from Arkansas and it was her birthday today, and their new dog Fetish. Chassler opted to stay behind in the chair and the rest of us went to the lake to swim. On the way, with Marie playing her animal-counting game out the window of the car, Barbara said she saw an elephant, a unicorn and three snipes and no matter how hard she tried she couldn't explain to Marie exactly what a snipe is. We stopped to buy crackers and beer at the place called The Little Store and not only did Greg emerge with a superior salami sandwich but Nan got back in the car and told the kids to hide their eyes and she'd have a surprise And pulled out an entire bag of lollipops. The beach was overwhelmingly crowded and we swam and jumped and dug and then Marie and Sophia started acted oddly awful, even Marie had a tantrum, she claimed Greg had ruined her castle while she was in the water (Greg's reactions to the kids are by now much more like a parent's than like a friend of the parents) and I blamed it all on the physiological effect of the lollipops. When we got home Chassler was sleeping with his head under the canoe with a book and a pack of Camels lying by his side, when we approached he started talking in his sleep, we never actually saw or talked to him, he just staggered out to the car a little while later and they all left, they invited us to come to their room tonight if we wanted a steam bath. Fetish seemed to scare Sophia.

 We put the kids to bed after eating noodles and vegetables, I cleaned the upstairs rooms and sat in the remaining sun reading the *Times* and listening to birds, I saw the cardinal again and many blue jays who seemed to be fighting. I really wish I would never have to sleep. It was such a beautiful evening that no one thought of working till after 8 o'clock. Then Greg and I got involved with a problem about the water for the washing machine because the outside faucet seems to run incessantly unless you turn the water off inside but that also turns off the cold water to the washing machine and we couldn't find the proper knob. Once we did and the machine was going the raccoons were already assembling outside, it seems like a lot of cat food gets wasted on the raccoons and skunks. I began writing a letter to Bill and in the midst of it Hannah called to say she was feeling lonely in Providence and she had no one to talk to especially about poetry and that she felt eccentric-looking and odd and out of place, she went to her high school reunion there which I thought was all too brave of her but she seems more able to do things like that than I or almost anyone else would be; when we talked about swimming she referred to the jellyfish as Puerto Rican men of war. Have I described the jellyfish we saw? They were all relatively small, all white and translucent, no more than six inches, pulsating or breathing with tentacles and purple and pink inside, that was the one we watched being washed up to the shore, yet it never was, one was a white circular thing with designs of pink inside, and one other was all white just a white blob with no other color, it was hard to imagine it as living. As soon as I hung up the phone Chris called, and talked to Greg, she'll come to visit him tomorrow. Now every day when I get to this point I feel like the day and night have ended because I've gotten to the point in the writing where I'm up to where I am. It's a great relief then for the obvious thing to do to be to look around and see what is going on. Lewis has just come down from working and is watching *Some Came Running*, there are no skunks or raccoons outside at this moment, Greg just went over to the shed but if he knew Lewis was fooling with the TV I'm sure he'd love to join him as they love to fool with the TV together. What I'm to do next is type out my notes from the Californian Utopian book so I can return it to the library tomorrow and take out some more, but it might be too late to start and hope to finish as it's my turn to get up early with the children tomorrow which is why I would nearly wish never to have to sleep, or that all days were days and a half, which is more at the tempo that I go. But children, and apparently most grown-up human beings, don't seem to want to do that, and why the fuck does the sun rise and set at this particular rate of speed, I don't understand it is too fast and it's the very sun itself that has turned me into the most impatient human being who ever contemplated its rising and setting, especially here where I can be in it. Or else I could write a poem, but only about all I see. On the bark of a tree stump today were massing female gypsy moths just sitting there. Maybe that's why l always think the moths are dead poets because they live such a short time and of course because they're around at night while I'm writing, oh I am way behind myself. Stephanie invited us to dinner today! And there was something Barbara said which it seemed important to remember, and include here, and yet I have forgotten it.

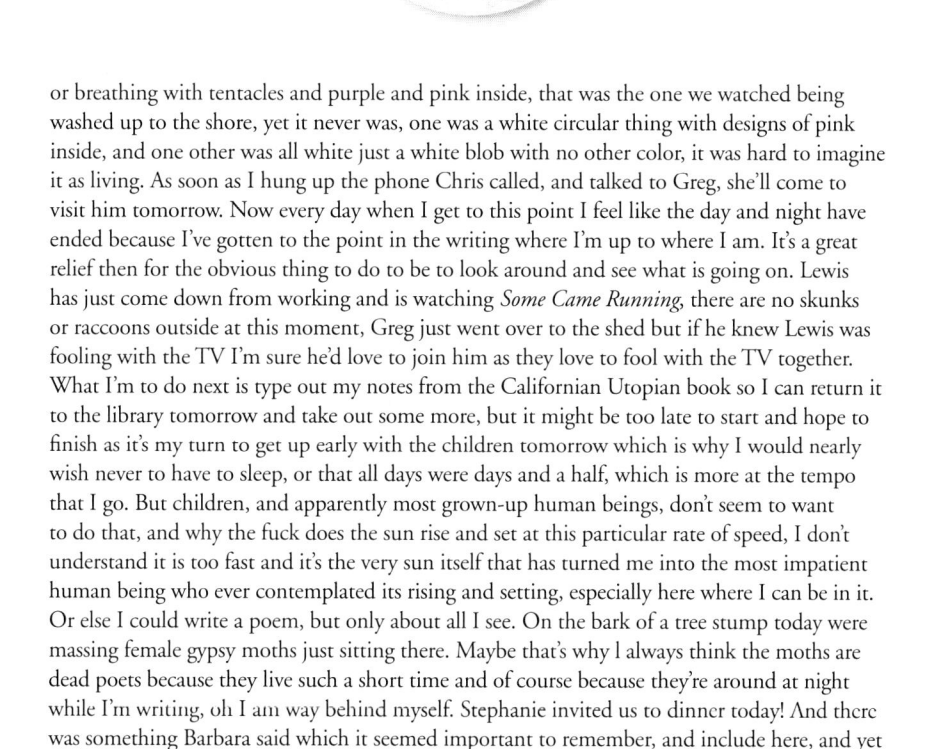

July 6

    I don't have the energy to write tonight and am not in such a great mood feeling anything I go on to say will be horrible or trite. The phone is going to wake me tomorrow morning and that anticipation isn't something to cheer about though it will be Chris telling me, in all probability, that she'll be on the 10 o'clock train since she's missed the 9 o'clock. Though I've about had it with visitors Chris is the only one I've wanted to come here and felt the need to talk with. Even missing the tranquil routine of the first week when there were no visitors with us and wanting to get that back and not have any more interruptions (further anticipating two more visitors in our brief two weeks remaining) Chris is the only person I'm willing to give everything up for, since she said it'll only be a day and night. I assume I'll try to make her stay longer. One month away too close to the city is a fraction of what I or anybody needs. Maureen, if you put your Xmas cactus in total darkness on the night of September 1, it'll bloom. So said Nan, an old friend of Barb Barg's from Arkansas as they and Chassler came to visit today. They were staying right up the road in a hotel Barb said she and Chass come to fairly regularly to take advantage of the steam bathtub cure, only an additional two bucks, she emphasized twice. Chassler stayed around the house to watch their dog, Fetish, as well as to just not go to the beach. I knew when we came back from the beach he'd be asleep somewhere and he was, lying in the front yard with his head under the canoe. "He's trying to kill himself," Barb said. Bernadette's had to communicate with the neighbors since they have a little girl, Stacy – though none of us are quite sure that Stacy is a girl, even though she has a frilly room and has dress-up clothes like ladies' hats and furs, which all the kids were wearing yesterday having a tea party outside in the bright sun. Stacy's mom and dad have invited Marie and Sophia in a few times to play which would be fine with Lewis and Bernadette and me to get them away for awhile but Bernadette and Lewis are a little aghast at the bad habits they could be picking up. For instance, Stacy's dad, Rex, or maybe it was the mother, smacked Stacy for some reason and Bernadette didn't like the kids being fed lunch without her having given permission, and she doesn't like the kids getting fed sugar which there was in abundance, Kool-Aid and marshmallows. Also, the TV in that house is on constantly with mom's soap operas. And in their big pool the water is over the kid's heads at every point. And both parents seem to be home all the time.

July 7

I remembered what it was that got said yesterday that it seemed important to mention, it was that Nan said if you put your Xmas cactus in total darkness on September 1st it will flower, but then she said that the cactus here looked like it was already about to flower. It's illuminating living in another person's house, here is a whole new way of living and a different set of books, it seems like a way to change. (To protect myself I say it makes no difference where you are at any time.) Tonight Marie said it was so hot in her room and I said can you imagine how hot it is in New York and she said you mean much hotter and I said yes much hotter and she said Oh god mommy, shrink down, shrink down. Then she gave a discourse on age and the ages of all the people she's seen recently, which had something to do with shrinking and heat. Then she said, Sophia always says what is a cup, it's like the skunk, I know the skunk is a skunk but the skunk doesn't know I'm a person and not a skunk, and I say to Sophia when she asks what is a cup, a cup is a cup, is that right mom? Very impressive for the new generation. Chris came this morning, it was an early morning, Greg got up with the children! I slept till 8:30 then I woke up and looked around and said my baby is missing! Greg looks wonderful, we are all very dark. People have three faces – one on their heads, one on their torsos, and one with their genitals. Lewis and Marie are the darkest of all of us, next Greg, next me, next Max and Sophia. The children were awful today. First Marie bit Sophia when she was trying to get a bird feeder away from her, really bit her hard on the arm, big teethmarks showing (maybe utopias are impossible), then all three children had relative tantrum at the beach, each seeking what the other wanted or craving to eat something that didn't exist. Marie tried to help Max drink some juice and spilled it all over him so that he choked and became covered with juice, then there wasn't any left either. It was the hottest day there has been here, too hot to be in the sun for long. I cleaned the downstairs this morning and put all the bottles and cans in bags and boxes and put them in the car. I tried to make johnny cakes but they came out thin and splattering. I think what I want to write is that I don't know enough and I'm beginning to wonder ... no I can't say that. We drove hot to the beach, first stopping at the library where someone had taken out all the utopian books just as I finally got my library card. I took out Aristophanes' *Ecclesiasuzae* (translated *The Congresswomen*), Marguerite Young's book about the Owen commune, and Lewis Mumford's *Story of Utopias*. Lewis took Rousseau's *Confessions* for Greg, *My Years With Ross* by James Thurber, and Castaneda's *The Eagle's Gift*. Lewis said the biography section of the library looked pretty good. I couldn't find *Voyage to Altruria* by Wm. Dean Howells but there were numerous books near there by various Howe's, including one by a Helen Howe who is not the Helen Howe we know but part of that family. I wish I were an Indian, even beaten down, instead I'm a German person with dark hair eyes and skin wearing my hair in braids and my face when it gets sunburned enough gets back what they call "pregnancy mask" which looks like your face is turning into one giant freckle, which proves you're white. Because I am a writer I lose patience with my children and act snotty toward my husband. If I weren't a writer, and weren't anything else, assuming I'm still belonging to the same race and am the same person, I'd do worse things than that. Now I'm really forgetting to tell about the day, I've become such a narcissist, so we came home from the beach, it was too hot and Max was tired and sunburned and I was worried about him and I made great and wonderful pesto in the miraculous machine but I had to make it with walnuts and 12 oz. boxes of Ronzoni fettuccine, in the store near the green, cost 97 cents each. Here, my favorite food has become lettuce and tomato sandwiches because of the lettuce, Marie eats plain lettuce sandwiches all day. We gave Stacy an avocado today and she got scared. She'd come over to play here on the stipulation, made by her father, Rex, that she "not come into the house"! After dinner we put the children to bed, which I guess I need not say every day, and Greg and Chris went to Chaffinch Island to watch the end of the day. This afternoon at the beach a most wonderful "yenta," as Greg and Lewis said, appeared to talk incessantly like a play for us. We also witnessed a fight and saw a congenial family. There are more people of other races now appearing at the beach. Now Max is waking up, he's done this a few nights in a row. Three raccoons, two gigantic, appeared at the cat food tonight, after the skunks had come. I think perhaps we must begin to feed the cats inside. The raccoons commenced to bicker about the food too – one would sidle backwards up to the other and when their asses hit they would make startling loud gurgling sounds – for a while it seemed like there was some proper eating order and one raccoon was waiting for the other to finish, but the other was too greedy and the one couldn't wait any longer, then one leaped at the other just as I was mentioning to Greg and Chris that it seemed like they all belonged to the same family, however I know nothing about raccoon socialization, housing or habits. What sort of place do they live in, Lewis asked. They're great looking and everyone wants to touch them. There's more to tell but I'll soothe Max now.

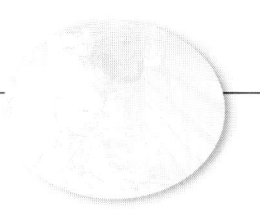

July 7

Chris is coloring polka dot flowers with silver leaves with Marie at the dining room table. Marie has no clothes on and suggested to Chris that she looks hot and should take off her shirt. We all occasionally watch the three, now, raccoons who come to eat from the cats' dish, the cats didn't seem to be appreciating the spaghetti with pesto anyway. It does seem to be getting out of hand. The black and white cat layed nearby peacefully watching the proceedings not seeming to mind. Chris and I had gone out to Chaffinch Island. "C'mon, I want to take you somewhere," I said at dusk. Visiting Chaffinch Island is something I used to do a lot last summer when I was here by myself. I haven't done it at all this time until tonight. As the air gets darker, the greens of the grass seem to become more enhanced, like tripping colors against the grays of the boulders strewn around, one of which we were sitting on drinking beers talking about whether or not it's unfortunate that her father doesn't talk much to her and her mother. I wondered if people like that are creeps or if there are some who are content to not say much, even if it's frustrating for others, like their daughters or wife. There were three older folk on another rock about 100 yards from us. I described to Chris how John McPhee in his Alaska book gives a sense of what it's like to be in a natural environment where there are no people for hundreds of miles and how that seemed to be the emphasis of his book, the freedom from neighbors. Our view looking north was a few houses on the peninsula stretching into the Sound and their lights coming on in pairs separated from us by an inlet on which assorted small boats were making their ways either out or into a small marina further west behind a small hill on which we could hear the group we passed on our way to our spot continuing their picnic. Directly west was the path we'd taken to get to where we were. Looking back in that direction boulders were strewn half in the low tide surrounded by straight bright green grass, all very still like it'd been steady for centuries. Looking out over the Sound, east toward Long Island, were blinking lighthouses on the horizon. A few hundred more yards of boulders and marsh extended into that expanse of water. Colors merged as the sun set and a mist settled. The sky was a pale blue-gray like a fresco. Stephanie didn't come by to ride Sean tonight like she said she would so we didn't get to solidify plans for this dinner she's invited us all to at her stepmother's. When I picked Chris up at the train station she wanted to see New Haven. I had to drive around a little but just made a circle around Yale and headed out of there. She wanted to eat lunch but I wanted to hightail it home. Marie can't draw a rabbit while sitting down.

July 8

We're having a heat wave, it's supposed to be being 99 in New York, and for many days hence, it's as hot as I think it could be here and too hot to be in the sun, we stayed in the cool living room and read books all day, the kids played outside, Max took a long afternoon nap, exhausted I think from so much hot sun yesterday, when we still couldn't accept the idea that it could be too hot in Connecticut. We didn't cook, we didn't do much of anything, it was the laziest day I think I've spent since I've had children. It's the kind of night when it would be great to stay up all night and sleep the whole next day only waking to observe that you are still you. It's true, Freudian psychology is evilly patriarchal, I was perusing the Mary Daly book. Every day we find a new book on Maureen's shelves that we haven't noticed before. Greg and Chris hung around in the shade and went swimming at evening, then came back and fixed scallops and rice for us. Michael and Steve called and said they would be coming up on Friday, really it is too many visitors. Now Rose has just called wondering if it would be imposing on Greg, who isn't here, to be picked up in New Haven at 1 a.m. I went out to the shed to look for him and nearly stepped on a raccoon in the dark. The moon is half. Marie and Sophia fought a lot before Sophia went to sleep. Sophia made a beautiful picture of all the people and letters that she knew – the only person who had arms was Mikey. I read Aristophanes' *Ecclesiazusae* this afternoon, a very funny play which unfortunately is more making fun of the women taking over the government than anything else, mostly for the sake of parodying Plato's Utopian ideas and also making some point about the dangers of paying people to serve in the governing body. But the obscene language is wonderful and there's a good discussion among the women about growing the hair under their arms. Now Rose has called back and she won't come till tomorrow and Madeleine called to report on her dealings with Arthur Cohen about the literary auction and it seems just like New York again and I just want, if it is New York, to write a poem, and if it isn't, even more so. Greg and Chris have returned and gone somewhere and it is a most hot night and all one is is a body and not so much mind as usual. I don't feel transparent today.

July 8

Tried to go for a late swim with Chris but once we layed our blanket out and taken off our shoes and began to walk into the Sound I noticed a jellyfish like the one Bernadette spotted that rainy gray day we all went to the beach. If it was just that one we would have said fuck it and taken a chance, but soon after I spotted another washed up on the shore. That did it. We went back to lay on our blanket and drink the beers we brought and talk. There were plenty of stars out and as it got darker we began to notice more. Chris didn't know any other constellation than the Big Dipper but she told me this Hopi Indian myth: A man built a ladder to the sky and the stars were holes where he reached in trying to get to the heavens. He ended up on the other side. I thought that sounded too Christian. There wasn't anyone else on the entire beach though there were some teenagers at the far end of the parking lot playing Doors tapes. The mosquitoes weren't any better there than they are here. We tried to ignore them as long as possible but it was really too much. Disgruntedly we tore up stakes with a final 'big' kiss. We both laughed , it seemed so lame. We drove around for awhile singing "Some Enchanted Evening" and all the other songs from musicals we each could remember, me basso profundo and her shrilly helpless female. She's made herself an ear of corn and sits in the kitchen presumably still reading *Gyn/Ecology* by Mary Daly, which she said is impossible to read, and when I looked through it before couldn't finish one paragraph at any point, except some poetry quoted. Rose called while I was out with Chris wanting me to come pick her up in New Haven at 1 this morning. Lewis and Bernadette talked her out of it for which I am grateful. Michael and Steve are coming Friday, this is getting nuts. A ton of hay is being delivered tomorrow. Gypsy moths come into the shack through the window held open with a half-liter Coke bottle. Twice today I've hunted them down. They're pretty easy to catch and I then fling them out. Chris left the door open for awhile and eventually it looked like an Alfred Hitchcock movie in here. Lying in bed we didn't bother with them.

July 9

    Here I am in the middle of a household, trying to write, that is about to contain seven grownups and three children. The state of our household, or utopian commune, at the moment is this: I just finished being engaged in conversation about women with Rose and Andrea, they were telling me exactly what they liked and didn't like about my writing and my person, why they felt William Carlos Williams was indefensible, why Greg was ok, why reading is "out," which men other men are ok or not, my most defensible position was one reads all the literature, but then it seems like the difference in our ages, about 5 or 6 years, prevents me from understanding that reading is not so necessary or important to poets at all. Now I'm afraid to go back into the kitchen for another beer, for fear the conversation will rise up again. The rest of the state of our being is: Max and Sophia are asleep, Marie is studying the TV listings with Rose, Lewis is upstairs working, Greg has escaped to the shed to work, Michael and Steve will arrive tomorrow, I don't know how this has happened. Sometimes lately when people talk to me I feel I am in a movie and not my real self, I feel like I am talking to people who don't know me at all, oh what a dull thing to say. We went to the beach early today because it's so hot thinking to get there when it's cooler, except that was difficult and seemed to take hours but we got there in time to observe the toddlers' swimming lessons which were sort of like *Sesame Street*, little imagination and conducted like a TV show. I had thought to learn something about teaching swimming to children but what I learned was that Marie's watching the swimming lessons inspired her to try all the harder to teach herself how to swim and by the end of our time at the beach she was actually doing it, swimming a few inches or feet by herself. Greg had brought Chris back to the train this morning and then returned here to wait for one ton of Canadian Hay (timothy/alfalfa, 30 bales per ton – $95.00 + $10.00 gas delivered plus $10.00 tip in cash), we haven't moved it from outside the barn to inside yet and we have to cash a check soon, we are running out of money though we got $4,000 in the mail yesterday, did I mention that? I also forgot to mention that Rose took her shirt off again, of course it's a pleasure to watch people be naked and Lewis and Greg took their clothes off today too, in loving imitation, and I suggested that when Michael and Steve get here we obviously must have an orgy, or whatever you call it, but then Lewis said that during an orgy with all these people I would be getting most of the attention, and that wasn't fair to him and Greg. I get pissed off when I see that Rose and people like Bob Holman and I can't remember who else don't care about my poetry at all, they think I'm done for, an old fart, washed up, whatever. Rose rather indiscreetly refers to the differences in our "sensibilities," Bob much more blatantly talks about my old-fashioned sentences and ideas – so it ceases to matter to even these poets what I do much less to anybody in the whole rest of the world, what a weird occupation this is. And in relation to the raging times, I would just like to say that all of us women have had our struggles with our upbringings and with the world and to be so hard-nosed as women to dismiss even other women for what are considered to be violations of the law, much less the dismissal of all other men and I suppose, often, all women who are heterosexual, I will never forget the coming back to New York and reading at the Ear Inn with Rose and being attacked afterwards for the sin of having children. I am growing more selfish every day, like all people who live in communes, and I only just want to be loved without reserve. What is the matter with me and what are compromises. What am I talking about, I'm only supposed to be telling what's going on. We had salad for dinner. I'm planning to accumulate all the quotes about sex from the utopian books for the first chapter or day. It's very hot, we swam, we hosed ourselves down, we took showers, we played football, we took more showers, and it must be even hotter everyplace else. I'm not supposed to like Kerouac, Williams, Dante or Shakespeare now. I think Rose should be forced to go to jail in order to read the *Greek Anthology* so she could find out about both homosexual and heterosexual love in ancient Greece. Knowledge is pretty random, again what am I talking about and who cares? For all my bad thoughts my ear is now stopped up which is good because it's the ear near the TV set which is on and I'm sure Marie is watching some horrible program. Greg says Sophia is a wild child. I fell asleep reading the Castaneda book this afternoon, it's kind of boring, I don't understand anything but now I've brought in myself again instead of telling what happened (both equally bad habits for writing). Lewis's back and chest hurt, he is resolved never to smoke or lift heavy objects again, so the 75-lb. bales will have to be lifted by us others, who the fuck am I, I didn't say that because I'd never mind lifting but because I was thinking about being a poet again. People are a little bit narrow-minded aren't they? Oh l will surcease (like an old-fashioned person) and only continue to say that I wish for and expect something, I might even call it transcendent but I also wish I'd never met or known another poet because, for the purposes of my writing and my life which is a little bit odd, there was never any reason but just loneliness to converse with other poets, oh fuck this stream of thought, I get in a mood sometimes where everything I say could be so mercilessly made fun of and it's much more illuminating to write just to write. I'm sorry, Maureen, for whom ultimately I am keeping this journal, for belaboring all this and boring you so intensely with what they call personal problems which take up a lot of space and aren't even written about very well, some strange song is playing on the TV now. Isn't it funny though to get tired of trying to put "things" into words. Did you ever have or want a mentor of some kind? There's a June bug on the screen, first one I've seen. We picked daylillies and creeping bellflowers for the table. I can't remember what influence means but it would be interesting to remember always what the moment is like cold water. They're watching *Victim*.

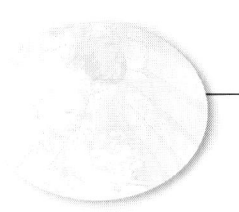

July 9

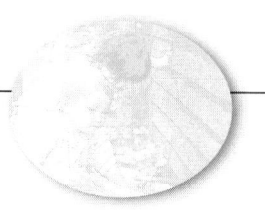

It's practically like a sauna here in the shed but I'm not complaining. I'd rather be here than anyplace I can think of or not bother trying to think of. As the days go by one after the other, it seems to me there's less and less to write about like the gentle passing of the days with its ease and vacation casualness is beginning to dominate the way these days belong to my life making the writing which attempts to define it seem like so much baggage. But I know too, to feel any worth as a human being, I have to feel like I'm accomplishing something. Though this journal isn't the most ambitious of projects it ties my day together. Sitting after dinner at the kitchen table, which has become one of my favorite times of day, I said I hadn't left the house all day then remembered I'd driven Chris to New Haven in the morning. We slept in 'the house' so as to be sure to be awakened early so Chris could get an early train back to NYC. I looked forward to being awakend by the kids coming into the room and jumping on us. But it was Bernadette poking her head in saying, "Marie Marie," that woke me up. Marie had snuck in quietly and gone to sleep on the floor next to us. Looking at me, Bernadette said, "It's 8 o'clock." Chris was her usual sluggish self in waking up meaning she doesn't until she has to or wants to. With there being trains every hour I didn't care too much which one she caught. I wasn't about to cajole her out of bed and suffer the wrath of her early morning surliness, the way we'd had to getting up so many mornings to go to our administrative jobs at The New School, walking in late every morning together, a shopping bag filled with a picnic lunch, maybe wine glasses. I felt pretty good making those appearances. Later in the day, more alert, Chris and I would have great discussions about how there are no happy couples or something equally as daring, pushed to the brink by the boredom of our clerical tasks. Waking up together this morning in Guilford, it was kind of clear that the room we were in, with the kids running around, was not the best place to make love so we just spent the time hugging and dozing off back to sleep with our arms around each other and teasing each other a little bit with probing feels. The 9 o'clock train took off, then the 10 o'clock. For the first time, Lewis and Bernadette and the kids were leaving early for the lake. I wanted to get out of bed finally so Chris could say good-bye to them. My gregarious nature had been tested with this visit. I missed the routine times of day the three of us (me, Bernadette, Lewis) had been sharing with the kids. I'd said the night before to them that the frustration for me of having all the kids around was that it took away from the time we all could be talking. Yeh, Bernadette said, we haven't had a decent discussion in five years. When I came into the kitchen, Chris had a cup of coffee sitting on top of the stove with the orange filter still resting on top. Some loving hugs and I pointed to my hard on. She said we could make use of that. It was exactly 11 o'clock on the New Haven train station clock when I screeched the Jeep around to its entrance. No time for any kind of good-byes. A block away I'd said get your stuff together and get ready to jump out. She used Duke Ellington's phrase, love you madly, maybe she said dearly, but I thought of Duke Ellington when she said it, and she was gone. I thought of having breakfast in New Haven but decided no half a block later and made the left turn past the police station to get back on the Turnpike. I forgot to see if the coffee cup Chris took into the Jeep was in the back. She looked real good with her feet up on the metal dash and gave the Branford toll collector the thrill he must be waiting for car after car since her long loose dress was pretty open showing most of her legs. After she said I smell something burning, and I did too, we didn't talk while I waited to see if the smell would continue. It didn't and we didn't either. I don't know why I have to feel there's something wrong when two people don't speak to each other for awhile. Making love earlier without saying anything, staring right into each other's eyes (actually I could only see one eye which was enough), was one thing. But as I was driving her to the train with us not saying much, I got paranoid about whether we have things in common. On the beach last night, she mentioned that I was quiet. Probably this all comes from not being used to living with a lover and just worry that every moment isn't idyllic. I'm glad when she says stuff like go write or leave me alone. It's a constant attempt to figure her and me out. She said she stayed the extra day because it took me the first day to remember how to touch her.

July 10

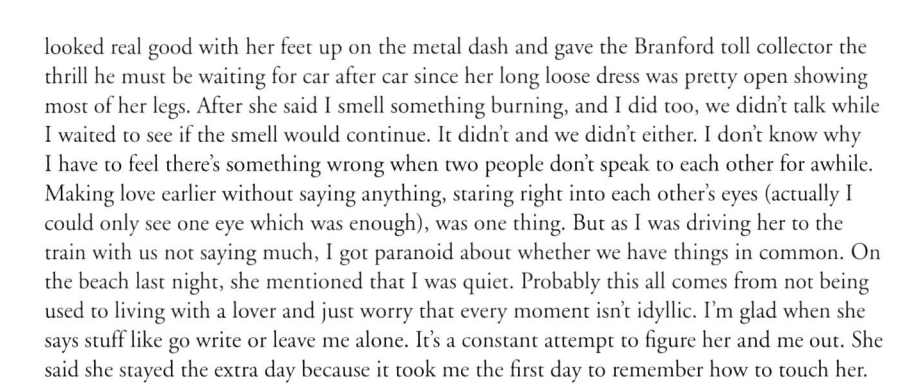

Everybody's watching *Alien* but me. Well not everybody, Rose and Andrea went for a drive. We ate Rose's health foods for breakfast, hung around till Michael and Steve arrived, weeded the garden, Michael took our pictures, Rose didn't sew all her seeds in rows, we couldn't figure out which were the weeds, we swam, ate dinner at the lobster place again ordered 14 corns then three more five lobsters clams and shrimps, it all cost 67 dollars plus a ten dollar tip for "Eileen," we went to the fair, Marie and Sophia went on the merry-go-round and so did me and Lewis and on a pony cart ride and then on a pony, we watched a man being dunked in the water Sophia didn't want to leave and cried all the way home. Put children to bed Harris calls he wants to see Dr. Ho and wants a recommendation then Dr. Ho calls he and Lewis talk about Schiff and then Berrigan who was unreliable and also about Chassler. We put the kids to bed, I walk out to look for my sandal it's a perfect calm hot night I notice the skunk up on the hill behind the horse's little range, I watch the skunk go up and under a rock where I guess he or she lives, I promise to show Marie the skunk's home tomorrow. The skunk's outside eating some cat food now. Michael is reading F. Scott Fitzgeralds' journal and Steve had to "proofread" *The Tibetan Book of the Dead* at Talking Books. There's a chemical fire burning at a pier on 16th St. on the west side of the city (of New York). Rose and Andrea are back and watching *Alien*. Rose told us about a fight she had with Jane de Lynn at the lobster place last year. Gary [Lenhart] wrote a great letter to Greg in which he refers to the "Warsh-Mayer professionalism" or something like that, talking about our reading and writing every night or all the time. Gary is really looking for a job and makes some mysterious reference to him and Louise having three children. I couldn't tell if it was a joke about us or a plan of theirs. We decided Michael and probably Rose could come to the hedonist's convention but that Steve and Lewis would have to run the ascetic's table. There's six hedonists right now in the living room of Maureen and Ted watching Home Box Office, well not six, and most of them are poets, there's as many poets as hedonists in that room but not all the poets are hedonists and not all the non-poets are not, necessarily.

Michael and Alice want to have a show of their photographs and artworks in the workshop rooms next year. Steve does too. It's going to be tricky to ask Michael to take Gary's job, and not anybody else. Rose says she'd like to have Steve's job. Marie's watching *Alien* too. There seems to be some heavy breathing on the TV set. Steve got very sunburned, we all wore some kind of hat. Suki met us at the beach, not before David and their son and two other boys came over to pick up the computer. Suki's just come back again from visiting her mother in the Boston hospital, she had been alarmed again but it turns out her mother will be ok she thinks. Then she Suki had her wallet stolen in a local movie theater. She was with a friend whom I think was named Lavinia, from Ireland. Suki won't be able to help us cash a check so it looks like we'll have to have money wired unless we can think of a congenial place or person in this neighborhood which I guess we can't. Did I mention we loaded the hay into the barn? I can't say we because it was all done while I was putting Max to bed. Steve helped too, after he found a pair of gloves. The bales are heavy to lift if you have to lift them high. Sophia had a religious experience on the merry-go-round, she had such a look on her face. I wonder if Greg has a good memory. We saw Linda Baxter at the fair. They had some peculiar pizza which looked at first like fried dough but it was covered with tomato sauce. I think fried dough only exists north of this part of New England. Barb has not left Eileen, she has just gone on a trip. Steve said he felt almost human he had had such a good time. It was a very gay day. I'll to watch the rest of *Alien* now.

July 10

The black and white cat's here being affectionate all over the place not wanting me to type. He'd paused at the entrance confused by the new screen I installed, but I coaxed him in with the usual cat calls and he figured out that the screen moves at the bottom where I can't fasten it with the pushpins I used everywhere else. I'd had it with the huge flying insects that made their way into the shed last night. The gypsy moths I could put up with, but these other beasts terrified me and convinced me that it'd be cooler sleeping in Lewis's work room. At 2 a.m. I walked over figuring he'd be done. I think Rose and Andrea were still up lying on the living room floor, but I made it up the wood steps and felt for a light in the room, cleared the bed of ashtray and books, and went to sleep promising myself to buy screens tomorrow. In the morning I was woken by Sophia screaming continuously. Get up out of bed after waiting for the commotion to end to go see why no one's done anything. I figured I couldn't be the first one up. Marie and Sophie are in their room on their beds. Sophia's diaper is full with shit smeared down her leg. Lewis had said yesterday that that's the first thing he deals with every day. I took a look into the master bedroom and Lewis and Bernadette are lying there naked and wave to me. That's much better. It's 9:30. As I'm headed out to the hardware store, Rose informs me that her and Andrea are coming to pick up some groceries. This means I can't spend much time in the hardware store walking up and down the aisles admiring the orderliness and the systematic displaying of all those faucet attachments and nuts, bolts and washers in different sizes on their metal pegs. I'm looking around for the netting, not wanting to ask for help yet since this is my only time to browse, and come to it near the shelving materials where a young employee is cutting pieces from rolls on a metal display holder. I pay and leave and cross the street to the overpriced food store to find Rose and Andrea. Stop at the drugstore to pick up the *Times* as I promised Lewis. When we get back to the house, Rose, Andrea and Bernadette start weeding the garden. They are figuring out as they go which are weeds and which aren't. Some thick-stemmed plants got pulled up which were possibly non-weeds, but since Rose had planted the garden with Maureen, if they didn't have any idea of what the plants could be they got pulled. I stood by watching with my book in my hand, a finger keeping my place so that I looked like I was just there momentarily and would be getting back to what it was I'd obviously been doing. It wasn't such a major job, though what was pulled ended up filling an entire large plastic garbage bag. Their efforts completely transformed the garden. At that point Lewis pulled in with Michael and Steve. He'd volunteered to pick them up in New Haven since I'd already made the trip a number of times. An incredible amount of traffic coming back at the toll booth, he said to me walking into the house. We all go to the lake, in both cars since there's so many of us. Eventually Susan Howe shows up with a new series of woes – her purse got rifled at the movies last night. She doesn't say goodbye when they all get up and leave and later, it turns out, she won't cash a check for Lewis and Bernadette, meaning she won't do the same thing for me, something she'd agreed to do a few days ago when I ran into her at Bishop's Orchard. So now I'll have to borrow money until we figure out what to do. Rose, Andrea, Steve and I got the ton of hay up onto the ledge above Sean's stall after we got back from a bacchanal feast at The Place. We spent a half hour at The Fireman's Bazaar on the village green. I blew 75 cents trying to win a homemade cake apparently baked and donated by the local citizenry. The calliope music of the merry-go-round was unusual and affecting like the best of Charles Ives. Marie and Sophie rode ponies around a ring, each pony led by a teenage girl. All of us watched *Alien* on HBO which didn't seem as good as it did in the movies the first time I saw it. What's wrong is that Harry Dean Stanton gets wiped out too early. Lewis and Bernadette went outside and later coming out to the shack Bernadette said I want to have fun not watch stupid movies. Michael took a roll of film in the first three minutes he was here. I thought that was inspired.

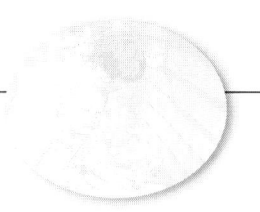

July 11

Steve is watching *Zorro* or something like that, Greg is reading either the *New Yorker* or *After Dark*, Michael's reading Lewis's *Agnes and Sally*, Marie's coloring, Lewis is upstairs. Rose and Andrea left this afternoon around 1. It was so hot today we couldn't go out to the beach till later though we tried to play some softball and football, then we poured cold water on each other. We are like sissies of the heat. The water of the lake seemed warmer than the air today, it's a giant bath full of people and one gets the sensation that it's the people who are making it warm and that if you swam to the other side it might be icy. We took pictures of everyone. Before we went there a program appeared on TV about Yvonne Rainer and her influence on dancers, she said that she didn't want to look at the audience, to draw attention to herself, to be a narcissist, to be special or elitist, she was always seen in profile or looking down. One of the most hateful things about incessant poetry readings is their narcissism, even the idea of introductions is narcissistic. Wasn't there some moment when we were all trying to change all that and how come we gave up. When I got up this morning Rose told me gleefully that she had actually liked the Poetry Project journal and I suddenly thought I had let her read it unedited and I had to warn her that if she'd read stuff that seemed like it might hurt somebody's feelings she shouldn't repeat it to anyone. She felt that things like that should be left in, I insisted that I always take them out and would have pursued it but I was changing a shitty diaper. All the children's digestions are awry. Too much corn, blueberries and esoteric health foods. Rose said after you "clean yourself out" like she did, you can really see how foods can fuck you up. Rose also said that the lettuce will grow again if we leave the roots in the ground, I am a little shocked at this idea. *Alien* was pretty awful with a horrible little monster bursting out of a man's chest in the middle of a dinner, then scooting or shuttling away quick to hide and grow in the spaceship till it turns into a sort of shark-gorilla-machine plus there's a person on the ship who sweats milk and turns out to be a robot which you find out when somebody gives him a karate chop and knocks his head off inside which is machinery and milk. Actually it sounds better when I describe it but mostly it was just a lot of suspense – people turning corners of the spaceship wondering if the monster would be there, endless scenes like that like car chases. Lewis and I persist in having the popular culture argument, especially with Steve. I don't understand these guys don't seem to want to talk, there's always records and TV on. If it weren't for the kids we'd probably get to talk around meals. Michael always has such a wonderful look on his face. Steve after his great mood yesterday got a little grouchy today. We went to the fair again and tried again to win a cake, I bet four numbers at once 11, 14, 16 and 27 and it came up 17, we did see a man win a cake. The kids went on rides again and had ice cream and we heard the Antwerp Boys Choir sing some madrigals and stuff. We saw a most inspiring sort of couple, I don't know what they were – an old man with a brace to help him walk on one of his arms, he had white hair, dungarees and cowboy boots and a sort of drawn handsome face, with a young man in shorts who smiled a lot and they were gay and affectionate and also seemed to know other people in the town. When Sophia rides the pony she opens her mouth, shows her big tongue and seems embarrassed that we can see her in such awe. Last night after *Alien* Lewis and I went outside for a while and when we came back in Michael had fallen asleep on the couch, Rose was putting the lights out downstairs, Steve had gone upstairs and Greg was gone to the shed, it was only 11 o'clock. I handwrote a few letters, Lewis read in the kitchen and then Rose got a phone call and talked a long time. We went to bed and made love noisily even though we were trying not to. I dreamt I gave the *Cold Spring Journal* (which has in real life had a manuscript of mine for their "next issue" for six years) a new manuscript to publish instead but the manuscript was a chocolate bar soaked in whiskey. Also I don't think I've thought about the *Cold Spring Journal* more than twice in these past six years. Then I dreamt I stole a pair of shoes during a spare moment in the midst of a very complicated schedule of picking children up from various schools. It was in Ridgewood where I was born. The shoes were size 7 (I lost one of my sandals). The night before I had dreamt I fell in love with Bill Kushner and we were holding hands on a new kind of subway. Rose and Andrea had a big fight today in the kitchen. Michael made an omelet for dinner and I made a salad. We are completely out of money, we were counting on some way of cashing a check, we are down to our change. Monday maybe we'll go to New Haven and Greg's friend there will help us. If not we'll have to ask Peggy to wire us some. It's not that we're out of money but that we can't get any. I had the feeling Suki must've thought our check might not be good! and we need a lot of extra cash this week so we can replace all the foods and stuff of Ted and Maureen's that we've consumed. Today I had to move all the medicines from the upstairs bathroom to a high cabinet in the kitchen – Sophia had locked herself in the bathroom, wouldn't come out and was playing with some hand creams, making a painting she said. That funny nursery school habit of encouraging children to work with weird materials, like making macaroni pastings and soap paintings seems detrimental. I believe in art materials. I'm worried about their schools next year, Marie will be in the sit in your seats and pay attention first grade and all the fun will be over, it's like you're telling children after kindergarten that their bodies are separate from their minds. I'm also worried about journal writing! It seems like such a ludicrous form, so strait-laced and what? It's been about six years now since I've been able to write straight and though it seems like time to stop and do something else, I can't, unless I'm to become an outright historian of some kind. In conversation I can talk about the problem and sound like l know what I'm talking about but I don't think I do. Everything's like an exercise, I can't stop writing. If I had a lot of nerve I'd wait till something became apparent to me, I don't have a proper sense of time. Proper? I don't know what to do is the problem. I set myself so many projects around when Marie was first born and then I did them, which surprised me and I've never had a clear picture of what I was supposed to do when I was finished. I have a great desire not to continue with so much recording, letter writing, etc., and to experiment again with some new form, but experimentation itself seems wrong somehow, but fooling with old forms doesn't make it either. Maybe what I need is a more long-term project, I've never worked for more than a year on a book except to revise later. Lewis has his novels he can fill his mind with. I must admit I love the prospect of this book I'm working on now but it also makes me laugh to realize that I'll have nothing new to read at readings next year because it'll take me so long to do it. I used to think the whole Poetry Project scene was so old hat, now the younger poets accept me along with it and they think I'm old hat or at best categorizable. But all the experimenting energy among them goes into the performance works which are not that good, so I don't get inspired. I get inspired by the straight poetry. Oh what the hell am I talking about. I just don't know what poetry is and I only get little glimpses when something happens like while I'm floating or swimming or when I see something a certain way. Or when I realize I'm alarmed about how the schools teach the children. It's not *Zorro* it's *The Three Musketeers*, I can hear it ending, one for all and all for one! Just like this Utopia! (How come men not only ignore cooking but also the need to eat?) (I love to cook but I hate being expected to provide meals for men because I'm a woman, or for children either; I'm not talking about Lewis). Shit I'm getting boring and long-winded, it must be because of a great desire for sex.

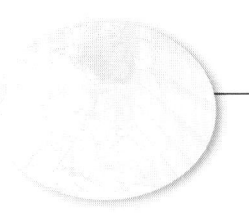

July 11

    What have I done? In four hours some baby is going to wake up, Bernadette says, as I get ready to leave 'the house' and head for the shed asking her to give me two minutes before she turns off the outside light. Her, Lewis and I have just stayed up watching *The Boston Strangler,* at each commercial commenting on how we can't believe we're continuing watching it but are unable to leave. I want to get back out here to the shed and write, but we're sitting transfixed in front of the TV trying to figure it out. I sense it must have more to do than just being seduced by the need to see the end, find out what happens. I wait to see him break down and it took the entire movie before he does. I'm wondering if there is some type of alpha ray or something that prevents us from leaving the control of the TV. Lewis still has the McDonald's Yankee hat on that he's been wearing practically all day. He wore it during dinner, came down from his work room in it and is going to bed at 2 a.m. with it still on. Steve disappeared earlier in the night with no goodnights or anything, just went upstairs and never came down, apparently disappointed that there's nothing to do but watch TV. It's true, we've been watching too much. We've even gone over to watching the regular channels, not just HBO, since we've grown disappointed watching *American Gigolo* kind of movies. For the second time since I've been here, I went out at night. When we couldn't take watching *American Gigolo* anymore and someone happened to mention sundaes, I suggested we go to Friendly's. But that's another horror, like a Norman Rockwell painting. Everyone in there is so immaculately clean they can't even imagine being soiled. The waitress is horrible to us, coming over and saying are you ready to order instead of hello. She does not look at us but looks straight at her pad and holds her pencil like it was a tree trunk. It seems that she is so stiff and seemingly ready to burst into tears if someone said the wrong thing. Steve defends her a little saying she has to put up all night with idiots. He asks for the Famous Friendly's Sundae. Only saw two Lacoste shirts. Then we drove over to Chaffinch Island, but neither Michael or Steve seemed too thrilled. We ended up just walking to some spot not even close to the water and then headed back to the Jeep. I can hear some animal in the garbage.

July 12-13

    Didn't write yesterday because after Michael and Steve left on a later train than they'd thought, we watched *Coal Miner's Daughter* and then talked for the rest of the night and made phone calls to arrange to get some money, here we are in a foreign country and we're down to our last $1.70. Yesterday we counted out $17 in change, I still have Steve's silver dollar, which isn't silver, in my back pocket too. Yesterday the sky was full of cirrostratus clouds all day and alto-cumulus at evening. We went to the lake where we again met Suki who said it looked like a bathtub. It was as crowded as the NY beaches were described in the *Times*: there just isn't any more room. The heat wave persists, now in its sixth day, the papers compare it to last August, but it is not so bad here, you can't sit in the sun a lot but the mornings are cool and beautiful and this morning was cloudy with sweet air and a good-smelling thunderstorm at evening. After dinner tonight we walked down the road and looked at the lily pond, picked Queen Anne's Lace, ferns and some purple flower that grows in the pond with beautiful single leaves. Lewis threw a penny in the pond, we saw a sunflower growing in an odd place off the road, it looked like a person, it wasn't full-grown, it was about a four-year-old person with its back turned to the road. The bushes or thick vines hanging over in semi-circles in the cultivated fields that Grace and I thought were gooseberries or something turn out to be raspberries, the other plants must be blackberries though there are no little buds on them yet. The migrant workers' shack is amazing at the end of this suburban and sometimes rich-looking road of houses – inside there's a fluorescent light in the kitchen, a bare bulb in what must be the living room and tonight some of the men were sitting smoking staring out the window. The rest of the people on the road have a different life from that. Stacy's house, from the front, is I think the most astonishing – a ranch-style house with funny crisscrosses on the windows that Lewis said made it look like a prison – a long skinny house, what is the matter with those people? We looked for more wildflowers in the field across the street and found milkweeds and many small purple ones I don't know the name of and little white asters. Yesterday on the way to the lake people were picking daylillies along the road and Greg quoted Emerson's enjoining us to leave the flowers in the fields. I picked three Queen Anne's Lace in different stages of opening up but they won't look at me. Sean had a bath yesterday and Stephanie says he needs more water, she had filled up his pail and he drank the whole thing down at once, it's partly because the way the new hay is situated he can get at some of it and is eating more, he hasn't been to the pasture all week because Linda said it was too hot for him. Last night we made rice and vegetables and I cooked the vegetables in sesame oil but it turned out to be sesame oil with chili and it was hot, it was great, it made me feel stoned, while we were eating it I decided my two best lines of poetry are: "If you want me back act bitter as a lemon/and hot as the foods that make me scream." There are so many little soldiers in this house. We had gotten generic diapers, 48 for five dollars. It was very moving in some way and a great pleasure when Michael told us about his trip to Montreal, he went there alone for the fourth of July weekend to get out of the city, he'd never been there before, I like imagining him doing that. The other day, without intending it, Lewis went swimming with his glasses on and with his wallet in his back pocket. I dreamt the words Terpsichore (muse of dancing), Stesichorus (poet of the *Greek Anthology*), and harpsichord, and then in that dream I watched a dance I didn't understand, it wasn't an everyday dance like Yvonne Rainer was talking about, it was kind of a boring lazy dance done by people who didn't care at all even about their dance. Then this morning I dreamt Walt Frazier came crashing into our living room through a kind of opening or hole, after he'd made a shot in "the auditorium" adjoining, which must be the field, and it was discussed that being

able to come crashing through this hole which was like the space of a counter or bar like in the kitchen of the Parish Hall, was a great feat and "Phil Jackson couldn't do it." I don't know what to make of this dream at all, except to know it must have to do with too many visitors, and something about the Castaneda book which I've gotten totally sucked into as if it were a cheap movie and which is full of holes and cracks and barriers and leaping, and ultimately I guess the dream has to do with problems of writing poetry and being a poet which is partly what we were talking about last night. This morning our money problems which were seeming so funny for a while suddenly became problems – we had planned to pick up the money Peggy was wiring to New Haven today and also go to the museum, it seemed like the perfect day to do it, it was cloudy and cooler, then we called the Western Union and they said not to expect the money till 6 o'clock so that blew our plans because of the kids and we decided to wait till tomorrow. We went to the library and got some new children's books, the remaining utopian books and Lewis took a Chardin and an Eakins book and I took a Walker Evans book. Having a library card makes me feel like we could stay here forever. In all the small towns we've ever lived in I've always felt so grateful to the libraries and wished after using them for a while that I could shower them with some sort of liberal affection and millions of dollars as well. The children's room in the Guilford library is especially posh and it practically distracts the kids from the books themselves, which reminds me of Sophia's new rhyme: "I came I saw I Guilford," forgive her. This was really our first "bad" day since we've been here. After the library we went to the Sound, not wanting to expend the little gas we have left going to the lake. There was no human being but two bemused lifeguards at the Sound, it was probably low tide, we couldn't even tell because the water was so full of jellyfish we barely even walked into it, it was hot and sunny by this time and the clouds were beautiful but the shocking thing was there were two young men scooping up jellyfish with a pail and depositing them in two small holes in the sand on the beach and ostensibly observing them, but then after a few minutes we saw that what they were doing was planning and carrying out their plan, to bury these beings alive. They did this for a while, no one stopped them. It seems like one of the sleazier ways of passing time available in Guilford though it was fascinating to observe the beautiful jellyfish all pink and purple pulsating in the little pool of water they'd made. All this time Sophia was having a tantrum and Lewis had stayed with her in the car for lack of seeing reason in dragging her screaming onto the hot empty beach, but her tantrum persisted and so we left, Lewis out of sorts by this time too. Sophia had gotten up early this morning, walked downstairs, poured herself some milk and drunk it, and then thrown up in front of the refrigerator no one knows why, she didn't feel sick she said. Home we put our change back together and finally Greg went to the store for our most immediate needs: bread, hamburger of all things, cat food, milk, juice, beer, cigarettes, coffee – what a tale that tells. Lewis and I had a little tiff about the relative importance of beer and hamburger, I claiming that beer assumed the greater role in one's life. Lewis had said this morning that running out of money made him crave sweets, I said it made me think about buying things, lots of things, it made me greedy, Greg said it made him feel quite content. Sophia's little tantrums, which made a hard day for us, have been becoming more and more recent and they always seem to be set off like they are for a two-year-old, by some transitions in the day – when we have to leave one place for another; she is definitely feeling dislocated and is regressing – she's 3-1/2 and shouldn't be so subject to them – and the only reason I can think of is the comings and goings of visitors, many of whom she doesn't know – she becomes friendly.

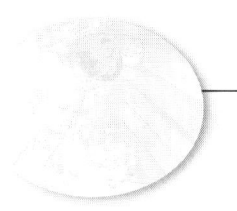

Also I think she gets up too early and gets grouchy, also her diet has been very different here. Oddly here in the country we eat much less of fruits and vegetables, because we don't have the great and cheap First Avenue markets and aside from the things that are in season here, everything is comparably fantastically expensive, and somehow harder to get. Just before our hamburger dinner I called the Western Union office and somebody I swear was named Rex told me the money was there in Lewis's name and we could pick it up tomorrow. One more thing about the children's problems – when other people are around, they often lose patience with the kids long before Lewis and I do and they do things like tell them to shut up or occasionally even give them a slight pat or slap or ask us why we don't hit them. This bothers me and Lewis a lot, it seems like if we've cultivated this patience, which is hard enough to do, that somebody else who's feeling hard put to bear the mishegoss of the kids should emulate that patience, more than anything else – after all, it's especially the only way to be with kids and other people all day long with any grace, no one would enjoy the spectacle of us shouting and beating up our children, as a part of social life I don't think. I explained to Greg how it is that hitting children, even if I found it conscionable on any other grounds, didn't work. Each life is full of so many days with so many hours I can't believe it, and there's so many people as well, and all these things and events, just think of all these things in this journal of just a month, and none of them are even particularly consequent, I doubt that anyone writing a novel would use many of them even for filler. My two main desires are to be high and to know everything. Meanwhile, the woman or a woman from a store in Guilford called Scuttlebut called to say to Maureen that her Irish flag has come in and she will hold it for two weeks, or for longer if Maureen wants her to. Then Sylvia, I think her name was Sylvia, called to ask if Maureen could suggest some needy poets who would like to appear in a film, what she needed, specifically, was a woman who could play an alcoholic mother! Now I could do that but it's in New York this week so after consulting with both Sylvia and Greg and finding out that the woman had to be old enough to have a teenage child, I hesitantly suggested Alice and suggested that Alice would at least know of someone who would want to do it. When she first called and I said Maureen wasn't here, she said, "are you a poet too?" Sophia and Marie whose initials if I were to write that way are S and M, just like Steve and Michael, chose *Beady Bear* and *Goodnight Moon* at the library today. And on the paper on which I'd written my Walt Frazier-Phil Jackson dream, Sophia drew a picture of a person, a long tall person who has two square arms both on the right side of her body and two square feet. I wonder if it's better with children to be able to notice every detail of everything they do and talk to them about them, or to be involved enough in one's own concerns not to. And with lovers. Sometimes I would wish to simply be completely on my own once again to do whatever I want without no one knowing anything about it, instead of this life where love seems to result in a test of entropy (Dear Maureen, there's a very weird definition of entropy in your dictionary, but it's poetic). But on the other hand, *Alien* is once again on the TV and right at this moment the little newborn monster is bursting out of the man after dinner, an image (not to see but when I write it down) makes me think maybe this is a good movie after all. Sophia talks about Patrick all the time and calls Ulysses "Melissa." They are astonished at Patrick's and Melissa's rooms and decorations and things. It would be nice if there were a place to go that encompassed children for a vacation like right next door (but not next door!). I look up at the trees and see that there's no way I don't have to begin to think differently. Max says bye bye. I'm scared. Lewis and Greg are watching Groucho Marx.

July 12

  I've come home from taking Michael and Steve to the New Haven railroad station and come back filled with revelations because I've gotten a little stoned and it's a good-bye scene and the whole ride back on the Turnpike the sun is at my back lighting up sections of trees and stone at the sides of the highway like it was dusk, which it was. Those trees were getting spotlighted with the purest filter any techie could find. It seemed like autumn when there were some red leaves. I go into the house after deciding to go talk to Lewis and Bernadette before rushing into the shed to put down these new startling observances. I'm eager to share with them some of these impressions. I can't believe it, they're curled in front of the TV as if we hadn't all gotten our fill last night. But it's *Coal Miner's Daughter,* which everyone's been kind of anticipating all week. It's almost excusable. I see myself getting suckered into watching while I'm standing there, so say 'it's good to be back,' to try to sum up what I'm feeling, and leave. Steve and I had our only good conversation of the weekend on the drive into New Haven and it got me excited. I regret that it hadn't happened before during the weekend. I think that one reason it didn't was that gregarious part of my behavior which aligned me with Lewis and Bernadette. As host, perhaps I put aside the fact that these are two of my closest friends visiting. Being a host can make you change the way you are comfortable with a place. Bernadette, Lewis and I have had so many visitors. We've all wanted, even loved the company, but we want to get our former pace back. The three of us have agreed on it unanimously, it's our own secret conspiracy.

  Michael, Steve and I smoke a joint with a final cup of coffee and load into the Jeep. Leaving the driveway, pulling out backward, Lewis and Bernadette come out to wave good-bye. Bernadette is still in her bathing suit. The scene makes me appreciate the few weeks I've been up here away. I'm hoping I haven't taken any seconds for granted. Lewis and Bernadette's smiles are so friendly and inviting.

  On the Turnpike there's a car stalled on the side of the road with a Pakistani-looking teenage boy walking around in a pair of blue shiny gym shorts. That also jars my senses out of context. I've tried to not think about the fact that there's only one more week up here. We've talked in the last two days about whether we should call Maureen to find out exactly what day they'll all be back so we can do what'll have to be a gigantic cleaning and restocking of inventory, mostly wine. Lewis and I finally went down to the basement this evening in search of tonic water which he wanted to mix with some gin. We came upstairs with another bottle of wine to open.

  I started writing a letter to Chris, right before we all got into the car for the beach. I almost didn't go but wanted to be with Michael and Steve while they were here. So far: July 12 Dear Chris, Hi, what's up? It's a normal Sunday here. Spending it so far like I figure much of the country does, reading the *New York Times* and taking occasional voyages to the kitchen. I ate Max's noodles and had to make some more. I've decided I like waking up with responsibilities as long as it doesn't exceed going over to a barn and feeding a horse, and a horse that doesn't mind breakfast maybe an hour or two late while his 'master' decides whether to get up or not. I tell what time it is by looking through the skylight at the sun and can tell pretty much what hour of the morning it is. Only once, yesterday, was the sun so far up that I had to bend my body to the other end of the bed to find it. It was yellow, reassuring. You can read the rest of my journal, if the first part you read wasn't so boring as to dissuade you, to find out what I've been doing since you left. More of the same. I pick out details and try to find something to say. I feel a little hesitant at revealing secrets, desires, etc., since writing is so public and I want to know these people a long time that'd I be exposing, me especially. No gossip or not that there's anything earth shattering, just ordinary couples stuff and how I have to regard them as a couple and how no one is really satisfied with the rules of behavior they feel compelled to accept even if they talk about their dissatisfactions.

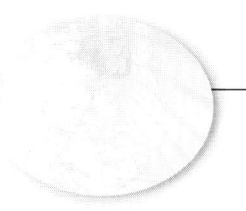

July 13

The only way I know what date it is is by looking at the previous day's entry. It doesn't at all resemble a prisoner x-ing off dates on his wall calendar. Lying on the couch a minute ago in some transcendent state, halfway between sleep and perfect contentment, I finally get up to get a beer. Dinner tonight was the first we've had that we haven't drunk wine. Everyone is feeling pious cause we're all broke and have the last few days been counting our change and putting it all together in a ceramic jar. We've counted it at least three times and had to figure and budget our last two days till we get to New Haven tomorrow to pick up the $200 at Western Union that Peggy today on her lunch hour wired up to us. I abandon the comfort of the couch and Bernadette's presence hidden around the open doorway in her study, and walk past the column where a number of Yvonne Jacquette drawings used in one of Maureen's books are hung. They are so beautiful in their detail and stillness, but are hung in too obscure a spot. You should place them more prominently, I told Maureen last year. Lewis is not yet typing upstairs. I return to the living room to pick up the Faulkner book. Its language and mysterious crazy narrator has helped in a realignment of my sensibilities. It's dusk. The final cheers of the soccer players and fans is coming from across the field and in through the screen windows. I grab the new Clark Coolidge book which came in the mail to Lewis and Bernadette a week or so ago and come over to the shed leaving it all behind me. Yesterday Marie called me her lover as I was holding her. Energetic Sophie. It is amazing how she can cry hysterically for an hour. There is absolutely no way to appease her. Coaxing her with a soft voice or gentle requests for her to be quiet or threatening raising of the voice all just make her renew her shrieks. No reasoning is successful. I appreciate the absolute destruction of logic, all geometry exploded with this three-year-old force in the front of the car. Everyone is doing their best to ignore it. Coming out of the library, for example, she says her shoe's untied. It's not, Bernadette assures her, and that triggers her off. She starts blubbering and doesn't stop on the way to the beach. When we get there, Lewis has to stay in the car with her to try to calm her down since he doesn't want to carry this crying child across the beach. Bernadette, Max and I go over and lay the blanket down on the beach. It is deserted except for two lifeguards sharing one seat and two strange teenage boys capturing jellyfish in a bucket and plopping them in pits they make in the sand. They then bury them. Why don't the lifeguards stop them? I can't ignore the hideousness of this genocide. Being that we're the only other people at the beach makes it even more eerie. Sophia's uncompromising behavior hasn't stopped so after a while we get back in the car and head home. She is still shrieking until we pull into the driveway. Pretty soon she's her other self.

July 14

Isn't it flag day or Bastille Day or something? Today for us mere poet-narcissists who are poor and crazy, it was the day not only of the lost postcard and the lost shoe, but of the money. First off, Lewis did this thing: he took a postcard he had written to Rackstraw Downes (who wrote a postcard saying he hadn't received word that Lewis had gotten his drawing, although Lewis *had* sent him a postcard saying he'd gotten it) out to the mailbox to put it in so the mailman would pick it up during the morning deliveries, but, when Lewis got there, there was one letter in the mailbox and Lewis thought perhaps the mail had come already. Then the postcard disappeared, Lewis may have put it in the mailbox anyway, though he didn't intend to, or it may have gotten lost (the mailman hadn't come yet and the single letter was leftover from yesterday), Lewis was also involved in putting jugs of water in the trunk of the car in case the radiator leaked again at this same time and we could not find the postcard. He wrote another but couldn't decide whether to send it because it would seem so foolish ultimately to be the author of two lost postcards, or perhaps three. After all we are not even so poor at the moment, only just out of money. So we got to go to New Haven only after getting the children ready for such a journey and the wind was blowing and it was cooler it became cooler and cooler as the day went on, I'm certain the heat wave is over and we drove to Chapel Street and Lewis went into pick up the money that Peggy had sent, then we went to the Yale University Art Gallery which is well endowed and I saw a dog from Toltecs and many other things, some Hudson River works and a nice untitled de Kooning and *No. 4* by Pollock and some Eakins. All the American works were by far the best ones. There was a Gauguin called *Adam and Eve, Le Paradis Perdu*. The children were good except for Max who was uncontrollable and ran around the galleries with no shoes on, trying to get into all the private rooms. The Toltec dog looked like the sunflower yesterday, Marie liked best a portrait of a girl by Sargent. She said the de Kooning was disgusting. She liked very much some old fruit paintings and some early American furniture. After that Greg took us to a nearby falafel place but it was a health food place and we had to wait a long time to get any of the expensive things to eat (it was called Claire's), we ate them on a bench on Chapel Street and then drove home, unable to deal with the children any longer. We had hoped to do some other things, I think especially Greg had expected to. Before that we had stopped at a gas station in a part of town which was all trees and small houses with backyards, looking quite wild. The woman who gave us gas called her father to open the radiator and fill it with water, I would've liked to be that woman living in that part of town. Home was the newspaper full of the day's news: another hunger striker in Ireland has died and today was the day of a parade by the Protestants celebrating some ancient victory over the Catholics, in Massachusetts the civil servants strike is going into its third week and no one has been paid for that long and the National Guardspeople are taking care of the nursing homes and stuff, in California they've told the pregnant women to evacuate before they spray for the fruit flies, Reagan's commission to decide the fate of the NEA has decided to keep it and not turn it into some kind of corporation (that's the Charlton Heston group), in England Thatcher, as they call her, was pelted with what they called debris, which was tomatoes and toilet paper if I remember right, when she went to Liverpool and the fucking *Times* published another in their series of hateful editorials saying something like the leftists and the rightists are both wrong in their talking about the causes of riots and in the midst of it they got a chance to say that riots are obviously not caused by unemployment and poverty because, they snidely pointed out, look at the riots of the 60s when government in U.S. was handing out huge sums of money all the time, people we know in England at this point are Helena and Steve and Marion. There was some mention of (governor) Carey whom Harry thought Steve was related to until he was all the more impressed that he was related to Harry Carey Jr., saying that in this country there'll be Reagan riots like the Thatcher riots very soon. Indeed, you can't mention mandates when everybody's disenfranchised. I'm reading a wonderful excerpt from Tommaso Campanella's *City of the Sun*, writ in 1623 envisioning hermetic knowledge type of utopia with big emphasis on breeding as the sociology. But this sociology for the moment is the supermarket where we went and bought lemons, bananas, peaches, red pears, cabbage, squash, corn, tomatoes, cucumbers, watermelon, eggs, cottage cheese, yogurt, muenster cheese, butter, milk, orange juice, bread, refried beans, garbanzos, generic kidney beans, canned tomatoes, matches, chicken, ice cream, pasta, saltines, paper towels – $44.15. Beer and wine at the other store. We met Stephanie who was bringing bottles and cans back to the supermarket and she told us Sean had lost a shoe today and was limping, we must call the blacksmith. Home we ate corn, tomatoes with oil and basil, cottage cheese with chives. Sophia chose dinnertime to have her tantrum for the day and I put her in her room but then Lewis compromised and said she could "sit in a different chair" as was her wont and she ate volubly or voluminously or whatever it is and they all had ice cream too and then the children went to bed. I read the interview with Steve Allen and Allen Ginsberg while nursing Max to sleep but before that I took him for a little walk and nearly wept at how beautiful the now cooler sun seemed and how quickly we'll be gone from these pleasures. Greg said tonight while he was reading *Light in August* I think it is, or some Faulkner book (which he says when he falls asleep reading gives him great dreams) that he began musing about our return to New York, he said I'll get dropped off first, I'll pick up my mail and come over to your house, then we'll go and get the Poetry Project mail, oh weeping. (I only dreamt last night that I was elected to the advisory board in some completely weird scene where I was tying ropes around a loft or somewhere and someone was asking me how I met Bob Callahan and I kept joking, oh I don't know how, you know ... and then everybody would titter too, I think it was a dream about "outsiders" which means people whom the normal constituency of Poetry Project just don't like, like including Jessica, however I was mad at this dream for being so entirely mundane, including sexual innuendoes). Marie wanted to go for a walk after the other children went to bed so I took her for a short one up the road a little bit, we looked at Stacy's house and then into the field to see the milkweeds which we hadn't seen since last summer and then to watch the horses in the pasture. The sun on the same small white asters in the field, if they are asters, looked like the light in the Manet paintings in the museum. Ever since I called Ray a virago in conversation with Greg I've been wondering if I am one, the dictionary says (archaic) a large woman, an amazon (I am seeming fat), a turbulent, quarrelsome woman, a termagant! That's just an imaginary being the Christians thought was a Mohammedan and was vociferous and tumultuous – a boisterous scolding woman! In the end that is like Ray. When Greg asked exactly what a virago is I said domineering! Oh ordure! I like the idea in Campanella's utopia that the king or whoever it is has to know everything about all the things and their nature. Later Marie set up a little desk and chair for herself outside my window and we were both working, she on a set of squares connected two ways like checker boards in different colors like the Albers paintings in the corridor of the museum. While she was doing all this she was saying to me repeatedly, this is a good place to work because if I have to pee I don't have to come inside and use the bathroom. Vincent Katz called to see if he could borrow drums from Greg, I heard Greg say, how'd you find out where I was? Then Linda Baxter called to tell us she'd be taking Sean early in the morning, in case we found him missing, but when I told her about the lost shoe – and she was going to take him jumping – she said she'd find out who Maureen's blacksmith is. She called back to give me his number but he wasn't answering. Linda said she or someone else would come and help us hold him down. It's nearly a full moon, two more days I think. I forgot to mention that the generic diapers are not worth their salt or whatever it is that you say and they fall off and Max shat in his (it's not even his) crib this morning this moronic morning where after that both he and Sophia had huge messy diapers and were simultaneously demanding food and I screamed and shouted at them and then couldn't think and cried and Lewis lost his temper about three more times today and shouted and poor Greg is having to see us shouting at our children all the time although he doesn't see me do it that often because I usually shout the most in the morning but I get so impatient all day when Max only wants to cling to me and won't let me read or lie down in the sun, then he has to climb on me and think I want to be nursing him and he won't sit in the car seat at all he wants to nurse the entire time we're in the car and it becomes if at any time in the day I sit down he is on me unless he doesn't see me. I feel then like I'm not a person. Greg said, when I described it this morning to him, that it was humbling to serve the demands of the children. I wonder why Sophia is looking so beautiful and acting so mean. Last night, in the course of trying to rewrite my *Alien* poem for the third time, I got obsessed with drawing a picture of "person" with three faces, real face, face of torso with nipples as eyes and belly-button as nose and rim of pubic hair as mouth, face of sex with ovaries and vagina or balls and penis, then I wrote: child, you have no sex mouth and little sex eyes, and, the folds of the belly later make mouth and hair then into a brow. And don't forget all the digits and the counting of the fingers, toes and teeth, and hairs and trees and corn plants and mailboxes and everything, in order to know everything. Bye bye door.

July 14

It's like a Noah's Ark of insects in here. I've given up trying to be humane about it, capturing them and letting them loose outside. Now I have to get the broom and sweep up all the ones I've swatted. Like practicing tennis, my backhand's improved over the last few days. The gypsy moths seem to be pretty much finished, now it's these harder bodied insects

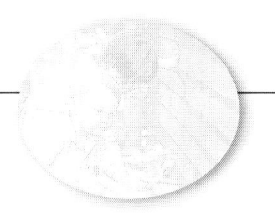

which make a lot more noise. They seem frantic knocking themselves against the walls and ceiling, which is some Styrofoam kind of insulatory material (like living in the inside of a coffee cup, Chris said). There's also a few daddy long legs and, worst of all, mosquitoes besides a few other species. I've tried not to stain the walls. There must be some hole somewhere where they all get in but I can't find it. Just knocked some gigantic bug about half the size of a hot dog off the outside of the screen covering the window right in front of me. This morning I got up in time to help Bernadette make pancakes for everybody. Marie and Sophie took theirs outside and ate them under the pear tree on the little bench. It looked like a little tea party. I was sorry to disturb their privacy and intimacy when I had to walk by to feed Sean. A batch I put on for myself became their second helping while I was out in the barn. Walking back I saw their plates refilled. Knowing there was batter left I didn't miss a step in my walk across the grass. At some point after, Sophie and I have a friendly chat in front of the water pump. I ask her why she cries so wildly. I am attempting to make her aware of what she does and explain gently how it drives everyone nuts. Her answer to why is, I don't know, but I feel something's been accomplished by having a real talk with this three year old. I even get her to promise to behave on the trip to New Haven we'll be leaving for in a little while from then and give her a little toy dog which I guess has been in the shed all the time. Bernadette's directions to the Western Union office are exact as we go to the other side of the tracks a little outside of the town. Lewis imagines living in one of the apartments above the office as we park the car in an illegal zone and he goes over to get the money. Then he comes out after what seems like a delay. His expression indicates to me that there's been a problem, but as he comes up to the back window he slides his wallet into Bernadette's hand and we're all relieved to have money again. The gas gauge has been on E the whole ride so we immediately start looking for a gas station and ride through town before finding one. A teenage girl in a yellow tube top and tight gym shorts pumps the gas and calls out "Daddy" when she needs to get change and because we ask for water to fill our leaking radiator. Her father comes out from inside the garage and he's very friendly. It's sad because he's starting to get old. There's stubble on his chin and he uses an old pair of checkered pants to remove the radiator cap. He tells us where we can get it fixed. Pointing. They have a machine there that checks the pressure and lets you know exactly where the problem is, he tells us. Lewis thanks him, I thank him and we get back in the car and find our way back to the Yale Art Gallery. New Haven seems so manageable, we find a parking spot right in front of the gallery and that doesn't seem unusual. Inside, the children are behaving. We wander the four floors gradually separating into different subsets to match tastes and pace. I feel like not allowing the kids to see the religious paintings. Why confuse them, I figure. But they're really so pretty, some with flakes of gold. That's Francis I tell them. There's hardly anybody else in the museum so it's not so obtrusive when Lewis and Bernadette are calling for each other, where are you, separated by a maze of early Americana. There's only one tired older guard on each floor, except a younger woman who's walking around seems more lively and not as depressed as the others though she seems to be suspecting us more than the others too. One guard sticks his head around the panels where a great frantic Pollock is hung and peers at us. We're all seated in the comfortable cushioned chairs in a corner in front of a newer de Kooning which Sophie likes but Marie doesn't. The guard retreats awkwardly when she sees Bernadette breastfeeding Max. What a wonderful place to sit. The three Rothko paintings in that room were a surprise favorite for everybody. I like that one, said Marie pointing out the big window. There's a terrible Picasso that reminds me of the daring and fuck-it attitude of Eileen [Myles]'s poem in a Boulder magazine at Maureen's, *New Blood*, which Lewis discovered had a transcription of a great talk between Steve Allen and Allen Ginsberg on Kerouac, which Bernadette and I subsequently read. The 'women' and I seem to spend a disproportionate amount of time in a Mexican room admiring the peasant sense of geometric ornamentation. On the same floor, Lewis and I had stood together in front of a large panoramic view of Mt. Katahdin at pink dusk, breaking clouds and a pond in which cows stand with their stupid grace, a long dirt road leading past what might be an inn, a small stone bridge across a stream on which a boy is lazily gazing, the road leads back and gets lost in the bottom folds of the mountain which comes right up from the surrounding lower mountains and looms, a power. "Nice color." Bernadette gets upset that a guard gives her a dirty look as we're leaving a floor. "What do people expect from children?" No one's listening while we're looking at postcards back on the ground floor. I'm telling about the time I almost stole the Jackson Pollock catalogue raisonné from the front desk at a Pollock exhibition coinciding with the four-volume work's publication. I picked the set up from the front desk, no one was there, and looked over at Tom Carey who happened to be standing at the exit. His first reaction is shock when he realizes what I am thinking, but immediately takes his own look around and gives me a nod. But I am too chicken and put it back down. After reading her entire folder of "Poems NY," her poems of the last year, I've chosen the following poems of Bernadette's for the next issue of *Mag City*:

>The Presentation of Fruit Stands in January
>I throw I throw my notebook
>Situation Vacant II
>On "Little River Farm"
>The New Malfunctioning Buses
>New Paper Not Meditated On
>Grace said she was watching the Miss America Pageant
>The Generosity of an Ill Wind
>Dentist Fiction

July 15

the moon is almost full, we saw it rising behind pink and yellow clouds while we walked down the Dunk Rock Road to the end tonight with Marie to show her where the Queen Anne's Lace grows, and we saw raspberries, two different kinds of bushes of them it seemed and we ate one raspberry from each kind of bush, one the normal green and the others the gooseberry semi-circles which are very close to ripe. Greg is watching *High Plains Drifter*, it turns me on to live beyond the nuclear family, quite harmlessly. Can I say that? The pleasures of today were: feeling the hot sun not so hot anymore that you can't bear it, swimming in the relatively empty (of people) lake (and turning to the sky and floating looking at the clouds, of the inspiring puffy kind you could imagine getting exhilarated flying above), real corn, watching Marie's pristine face, kissing germanic Max, measure the sunflowers, eat very hot rice and vegetables, drink lots of wine and walk Marie down the road. Greg and Lewis are kind of stodgy about excesses though Lewis loves an excess of work and Greg loves pleasures I am certain, but I haven't told anything of the day, we did this and then we did that and then that happened and then she and he were that way and then she oh and so on. There was some sort of sex scene in *High Plains Drifter*, I didn't see it. Last night we watched part of a mammoth TV movie about battered wives, it was all-engrossing except you couldn't continue to watch it it was so awful. The night before we had had a long discussion about various movies ending up with all of us trying to figure out the name of the Bunuel movie *Belle de Jour* which we finally learned because Lewis went upstairs to find a book he remembered seeing on the shelf and he passed it down to the living room through the great hole, *Belle de Jour*. Lewis had said *Bonjour Tristesse*, which wasn't bad. I was fixated on *Viridiana*, it's funny when we have these conversations it's almost like showing off. Today's loss was the last page of *All My Friends are Going to be Strangers*, it just disappeared, no one can find the page, then Lewis said all the books he's been reading have been falling apart, Lewis couldn't find his shorts either and I still can't find my other sandal. Last night Greg went out to the barn to see Sean late and raccoons attacked him, this was right after the wife-beating movie. It took 2 hours and 14 minutes to roast the chicken for tomorrow's dinner but I have a feeling it'll be eaten before then. You see if you don't try to remember and tell everything in order everything will get told anyway which is a pretty specious and elementary thing to even bother to say. When we came back from our walk Peggy had called so I called her back and we talked a long time. Lewis and I and the rest of us blood relations will leave on Monday by train and then Grace or Lewis will drive her car up here to pick up our things and Greg will stay till Maureen and Ted and everyone get back. The Castaneda book keeps saying, as they always have, that having children makes holes in your self, in your fucking luminosity, the cats like to be patted, now one's climbing up to me – to distract the cat I gave it the chicken's heart to eat. Seven Queen Anne's Laces pink at the beginning with purple hearts in the center, some fallen away, will never convince me that royalty is anything but to be sneered at and all these utopias so stupidly seem to keep up some idea of royalty or the lack of it. Why do I write so much, do I consider myself some kind of royalty? Max dumped all the cat food out on the ground, everybody's eating it now. The skunks have already been here, why do I love you? Maureen's chair squeaks like a cat when you lean back. I even like the wind blowing on my face when we ride in the car (its poor radiator), it takes so long to learn something. Oh vacation, I dreamt last night I was living in a donut-shaped commune and when I woke up I realized I had to ask Grace some questions, formally, in writing. Now I've given the cat the neck of the chicken, all roasted with soy sauce on it. Wouldn't it be a measure to have everything all the time and all knowledge and be quiet.

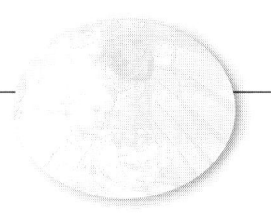

July 16

Full moon, Ray can't sleep, there's a partial eclipse at midnight, Greg is under the weather, I saw luminous eggs at the supermarket. Max awoke at 5:45 this morning, had torn off his generic diaper earlier and his sheet was wet and he wouldn't go back to sleep or be quiet. Then Sophia came in at 6 o'clock to amuse him, I got up at 6:30 complaining and spent the morning in the hot sun reading the Castaneda book. I was rude to my children and wouldn't let Marie and Sophia go to visit Stacy till much later. Max was acting erratic and clinging to me. When Lewis got up I took a nap and dreamt about my name, at least Lewis was calling it when I woke up. Greg feels sick and is not himself as they say. I took photographs of Marie making rainbows with the hose. It's sad to be leaving so soon but a warrior is never sad. We went late to the beach where the clouds were more stupendous than ever and another pleasure is to float watching them, the lake was almost completely still. As a child I couldn't bear criticism, I think I remember every criticism that was ever leveled against me including: there is no such thing as almost completely (I had said a peninsula is a body of land almost completely surrounded by water). I've been trying to put the house in order, I hope we haven't made it too disorder! – just by our being here. And though Sean (Linda spelled his name that way in a note) needs to be re-shod, I cannot seem to reach the blacksmith, he is never home. And he still seems to be getting at the hay. This was a passive day. Went to the supermarket – I think Finast's is a power spot, there are no fluorescent lights in it – and bought Romano cheese, cat food, mayonnaise (actually generic salad dressing!), laundry detergent also generic, bread, Pampers to use at night to keep Max from pulling them off, juice and lemonade. Got real corn, real carrots, real beets and somewhat real tomatoes at Bishop's. Drove back home and felt silly all day, ate chicken sandwiches, corn and tomatoes for dinner. Had chicken for breakfast, peaches plums and saltines for lunch. Put exhausted baby to bed, cleaned up the outdoors, watered plants, washed Max's sheets and blankets, took out garbage – Greg has put rocks on top of the garage cans, successfully. Walked out on the road and got inspired to do funny exercises. I've got four more library books to at least scan before we leave. Had one page left in the Castaneda book when Ray called, she and Harry are going to Vermont to visit with sister Suzie for a week, she asked me how I was doing with the laundry, we discussed packing for vacations, I told her about the lobster place and how I wished we could buy a house here (I didn't mention I really want a shack). I feel bowled over by the book and it makes me feel like I am a silly person which I of course am, but I'm really a poet that is all. Finished the book, then a friend called for Ulysses. I tried the blacksmith and Peggy, not home. Even poetry is silly these days, look at all these silly pretentious books: *Knowledge* by Michael Heller, *The Eyes Don't Always Want to Stay Open* by Philip Lopate, *Amerik Amerikh* by Geo. Economou, *Tear to Open* we won't mention that one. Then again there's a lot of good books too: *The Collected Books of Jack Spicer* (I don't like titles like *Diving into the Wreck*), *Sojourner Microcosms*, *As We Know*. Poor Fanny, we met Lavinia on the beach and she told us Mary Manning had suddenly to have an operation and Suki went to Boston again (Fanny'll be back this week) but Lavinia went into every single detail of Suki and Fanny's mother's problems, it was excruciating, poor Suki too, maybe Lavinia is lonely or something. Poor Hannah I wonder how she's doing. My poor ears are all clogged. Poor Greg's stomach. Poor Max he has to be two now for a while. Poor Marie she won't have anyplace to swim for the rest of the summer, just when she's learned how. Poor Sophia she has to be the middle child (I don't believe in that). Poor me, Lewis and Greg, we have to go back to New York after living in this veritable paradise. Especially poor me, I think Max is waking up. Poor Sean he lost a shoe. The poor cats they can't make up their minds about anything. Also the poor moon – I'm only fooling.

ADDENDUM A:
Things we've used up (to replace):
Pickles
2 cream cheeses
toilet paper
cheddar cheese
4 bottles of wine and some beer
2 beef raviolis
1 can of apricots
Romano cheese
lemonade, grape and orange juice
1 can espresso
Raisin Bran
1 box of pancake mix (rich earth)
2 refried beans
laundry detergent
sweet butter
yellow index cards
white paper
onions
1 spider plant that got knocked over & though it seems to have survived and is sprouting something, all the leaves are gone

July 16

Last night I went out into the backyard to look at the moon. When we first got here it was in its first quarter, now it's almost full. I heard this animal distress kind of calling. I followed the sound to the wood pile and looking in tried to see what was going on. The cries continued and I realized it must be a raccoon or skunk stuck in there. I ran back toward the house to get the flashlight and as I got to the door a skunk was right there. It didn't budge as I ran up. Stepping around him, I entered the house, grabbed the flashlight and ran back outside. Flashing the beam around the pile I saw a gray fluffy tail. I started to move pieces of the firewood to free the little critter. When I got close to it, it started getting nervous and burrowing deeper into the pile. At that point the wood all rolled back into the spot I was clearing and the cries of the animal stopped. I figured it must have been crushed. Now a little more desperately I began removing the chopped wood, throwing pieces to the ground. Once I got back down a few rows I could see it again and it started making its screeching noise again. By the time I was down to the last layer I could tell it was a young squirrel and I moved cautiously so it wouldn't scratch or bite me. When I took off the last piece of wood on top of it, there was a sustained second of mutual recognition. It paused staring at me before it realized how vulnerable it was, leaped at me bouncing off my shoulder to the ground and I ran back to the house shaken up. Bernadette was on the phone so I couldn't tell her of my adventure.

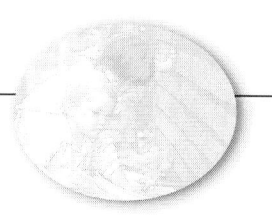

 This morning I couldn't wake up. It seems I'm a little sick. All I did today was lay on the couch reading Faulkner and sleep in the afternoon after everybody went to the lake. Getting up to eat supper was difficult and summoning up the resources to do my job of cleaning up after came from deep in left field somewhere. I didn't want to ask to be excused. Then, gladly, back to the couch for more Faulkner and the gradual sinking of the sun out the window. Everybody asked me how I was feeling when they got back from the lake. Bernadette had one more page to read in the new Castaneda (she pronounces it with the Spanish rolling n) book when the phone rang, Lewis' mother, and they talk for awhile and she calls Marie over and I hear Marie say, 'I've learned how to swim, I can put my face in the water.' Lewis, typing upstairs, isn't called. The living room is a mess. Earlier in the day I'd asked Marie to pick up all the little soldiers strewn around, but she didn't feel like it. Cleaning up, everyone says, shouldn't take so long. I think the plan now is for Lewis and Bernadette and the kids to take a train back to NYC on Sunday while I stay behind to take care of the animals until Maureen and Ted get back probably that day or Monday. Lewis will drive up with Grace on Monday to pick me and all their stuff up. Everyone's sad about having to talk about that kind of stuff. Bernadette even conjectured that my stomach disorder could be due to that. I don't mind so much having to leave here as where I have to return to. It seems like I've been gone an incredibly long time and that my whole NYC life is so far away. Bernadette has to call Peggy again to wire up more money. Fortunately we've discovered that Peggy can do it by phone with her charge card and there's a Western Union office in Guilford. Lewis and Bernadette report that the town green is going through another metamorphosis as the annual Crafts Fair begins to set up. Streets have been rerouted. Booths for clothes for sale as well as art presented by the Guilford Art Council have begun to be set up. We're going to miss the harvesting of all the local fruits and vegetables. There's a minor eclipse at 11:45 tonight but I'm waiting for a call from Chris before rejoining Lewis and Bernadette in the house to go out and watch it. Black ink cloud shadow leaked on the moon.

July 17

 I'm all screwed up again. I thought I'd decided to write one utopia, in the formal utopian questions and answers beginning with a conversation between two friends, one utopia which would be a farce, keep the Poetry Project journal separate, and also write a series of sex poems.

Now I can't figure out if I can do any of those things and on looking at my "sex poem" of last night, I see it needs a lot of work (I think I am making a joke here). I'm discouraged at having gotten so little done this past month. But beyond all that I dreamt last night that Max was a sado-masochist! He was an adolescent child being snotty to everyone and cocky and somehow he was diagnosed as S&M (Sophia and Marie? Steve and Michael?) by a doctor who then handed me a plateful of millions of different kinds of pills spilling over into each other, there was no way to tell one from the other or their purpose, the doctor was being very attentive to me, Max had a sunburn on his back it was all red which was one of the ways they were "proving" he was also masochistic (besides being overtly sadistic). At one point he was spitting water at everyone the way Greg and Marie do in the lake. A juvenile delinquent. I made some notes about this dream early this morning and though I can't read them they make reference to Moses Berkson. Evidently I woke up and told Lewis I'd had a nightmare but the dream seems to have more sense of humor than that. In another scene I was walking back to this house and met two friends who were on their way over, we encounter a heavy oppressive wind which makes it impossible even to walk against. I gesticulate and burn one of them with my cigarette. Then I see, in some magazine, an article with pictures about some British royalty (a relative of?) among a group of animals a little like penguins in the way they mass, but they are animals that wear hoods like Ku Klux Klanners and they look a little like Catholic priests in vestments (after this I'd made a note: "my long talk with slick stupid doctor," so this all must've been the same dream). I don't think I've ever slept so heavily and almost sluggishly as last night. We had tried to watch the eclipse outside but it wasn't beginning yet, we made love a little hurriedly thinking Greg, who was on the phone with Chris, might walk out and see us in the light of the moon fucking under a partial eclipse, I could see and smell the grass as I can smell the skunks now (I took a picture of them in the dark and they leapt at me). We went upstairs to bed but I couldn't sleep and wound up being able to see the whole eclipse out the bedroom window and as a result of that or my poem or sex itself I stayed awake thinking about sex for what seemed like hours. The eclipse was partly covered by momentous moving clouds and I had to keep slipping further and further toward the foot of the bed to see it. Oh now I remember even more of the dream, there was a moment in it when I said to myself it must be embarrassing to Max to have a mother with nipples like these and I saw my nipples were elongated like the Mexican statues in the Yale museum, there was a connection to Katie, that Max was Elio, and to Greg. I nearly called Greg Max and Max Greg the other day, if that's simple it surprised me nonetheless. But I've told now nothing about the day, just about myself. We traveled out to the lake beach again, by the time we got there the radiator was overheating already, hissing, we saw – as we told Greg later who didn't come along – that the beach was overrun with FBI agents and gay couples (men). Of course that isn't true but it was fun to speculate about the two FBI agents who were sitting next to us, for a long while we'd decided they were mute but when they got up to leave one of them said, "a hot day, isn't it" and then the other one said "yeah." Now that sounds like an agents' conversation to me. I was the one who thought they were gay because one of the men had an earring and that is so rare in Guilford. In fact I was watching him sleeping in the sun and could easily note he was a narcissist. His cohort had a handlebar mustache and was a bit out of shape. Their gear was bland but hip. The other "couple" had tattoos all over them and spoke in a fey way and had a heterosexual friend, also with tattoos, a man I've seen before on the beach with his child. I also overheard a fascinating set of "making conversation" between a young man and woman who seemed to be on a date. Marie swam as she's never swum before, taking a few little lessons from a 7-year-old girl named Sarah who was brashly competitive and kept saying "I can't do this can you do that" etc. Sophia was a little bit out of it, Marie tried very hard to float, Max ran into the water repeatedly and dumped pails of water on himself on his own. Lewis and I talked about all our friends and Carlos Castaneda. When we got home Greg went to Madison to pick up the money his mother had wired to him to someplace called the Jolly Rogers drug store, or something like that. I made sauce for pasta and pea soup for tomorrow, I don't know why, I've had no appetite for two days, either empathizing with Greg or (and Lewis said his back aches today! and then I watched him swim out into what Marie and Sophie call "the deep" but then I figured if he suddenly couldn't move one of the beautiful lifeguards would save him). Now Lewis and Greg are watching *The Godfather* and we have a date later to watch *Cape Fear*, which Lewis says is a great movie. Marie and Greg had a date tonight, they went walking and to watch the girls' soccer game across the street. It was another pristine night, I mean evening. We're trying to make plans about when and how to leave and we can't decide if it'd be a total hassle for us to still be here when Ted and Maureen and family return. We'd thought it would be and that their returning after a long trip, they'd want their house to themselves. And especially their crib. Now we are in a quandary because Grace can't come up till Tuesday, however, perhaps we'll take the train and Lewis will drive up later to pick up our things. Now Greg's decided to go to Friendly's for ice cream. Tomorrow we'll clean, shop and swim and get ready to leave back to the tight old city to write heat of August poems, deal with in-laws, listen to Ted, walk to the park, answer the phone, do all the Poetry Project work I haven't been able to do here where the windows are so comfortably low, here full of mirrors in the trees (Gregory the hangman?), back to the fucking elevator so far from the real ground and so phobic, you could imagine someone actually creating your life for you if you live in somebody else's house, your life is so temporary anyway, I can imagine imagining that I will get my tight close house in order finally yet I'm sure I won't be able to in that way, I'd need a crew of six to do it, I need warriors, I want to be a sorceress, I'm sorry forgive me but magic, the country, coincidences, the full moon and the books I am reading plus writing are all conspiring to make me feel this way plus the skunks raccoons rabbits horse (Lewis just said "I've had it with lobster," Greg came back with chocolate chip and strawberry) and their houses and habits. I had written last night in the midst of my lunacy, "the earth is a planet," well one has to write something like that down once in a while. I hope it rains, I hope it rains I hope it rains I want to go home in the rain in the style of weeping but what the fuck. When we were driving to the lake up 77 I was looking out the window as always and not noticing I noticed I was thinking I was about 26 then when I thought I was 36 I said to myself I think I will be 56 and doing this same thing and it will feel the same to me in my body. Yet each ten years is so much to us as children and for the children and ten years ago I had none of these children, I was writing *Memory* and working in Massachusetts for the summer and walking five miles to the theater when I wanted over the back roads where you saw not only deer but veritable meteors (the Mills Brothers have been together 56 years) and getting my first dose of the fear that obsession with writing and driving oneself can create and it was that 10 years ago that I read the first or second Castaneda book, I remember lying in a hammock in that wonderful house in Alford, Mass. which was designed so when you took a bath you could see into infinity in diamond-shaped mirrors on each side of the bathroom walls, I didn't I am still looking around for the same things still in other people's houses, or rented places, I am jumping around like deer and jackrabbits assuming that I am lithe enough to be learning everything, not to remember everything, or else I have a plan (to be 56). I'm stunned by the connection of this journal, which I thought I began just instinctively to keep Maureen and Ted up to date about all the goings on in their house and environs, with *Memory* which was done July 1-31, 1971. Well what of it Bernadette, don't be so precious, it's matter. But a month in the country, in any year, no matter what, is nothing to sneeze at (is that the phrase?). I still know, no matter what Bill Berkson and I have talked about, that there is something to be learned from the country, to be used and gotten but this life is always so up in the air and one never spends all the time you need to learn those things, I mean I'd rather be Uncle Bud, I would, but I have to begin to remember, if I can remember anything, that I come from Brooklyn and that is all and I married a man who comes from the Bronx and that is even more all. So when I dreamed of years past I was only a little bit off, I was knowing what I was dreaming. Now I've gotta go keep my date and watch *Cape Fear*, Love, Earnest Bernadette.

July 17

Back from an after-dinner walk with Marie through the fields. We strolled on a worn-down path between blue, white and yellow wildflowers and Queen Anne's Lace and assorted weeds that leads to the soccer field behind the grade school. A team of young boys was playing coached by older guys, one of them playing. Four or five adult spectators were laying on the grass kind of paying attention, but we walk past all that to where I spot another path. This one must lead to another field since there are even louder shouts and cheering coming from over in that direction on the other side of a grove of trees. We walk up there and it's a full-scale game with 7-8-year-old girls in uniforms. There are plenty of spectators at this one, all parents presumably with some fathers on the sidelines shouting continuous directions. It's depressing as the players are seriously competitive. I take a quick look at the crowd to try to spot someone it'd be interesting or even amiable to talk to but they all look unapproachable, so protected or fat with their fat black dog. We return to the swings taking note of all the plants and look in the stream. I'm trying to remember what it was like being Marie's age and having an imagination, making everything adventurous and adding excitement and possibility to what's already provided. There are a few ancient trees which rise above everything. This would have been the spot to watch the eclipse last night, except the mosquitoes are already driving me nuts. Marie comments, "I like trees a little." We then circle around past a large pond covered with lily pads, white flowers closed in the dusk and through the large farmland of Bishop's Orchards planted with raspberries and squash. Meanwhile I'm worried some horrible guy is going to approach us and punish me in some horrible way for trespassing, but there's no one even near these fields. We make our way back to the road and some bicyclists come rolling past. We used to call these punks, I say to Marie handing her a cattail seed head I've broken off for her. I haven't seen one of these in a long time and it's instantly nostalgic. When we get back from our walk, Lewis is at the door acting like a perturbed father to the guy bringing his daughter back late from a date. I sing "Wake Up Little Susie," while I'm pouring some grape juice for Marie and opening a beer for me.

I stayed home again this afternoon to relax and recover more from whatever it was that was wrong with me yesterday. I finished the book that I didn't finish last night. Then I waited for everyone to come back from the lake so we'd all go pick up the money I'd had my mom wire up to Madison. I figured they'd all like to go somewhere new. But when they got back they'd had enough driving so I went by myself in the Jeep. Madison is about one step up in activity from Guilford. There was a movie theater and a more commercial center. I walked up and down a few times wondering if I was being noticed. There was even a copy of the *Soho Weekly News* at the newsstand. I would have bought it if there'd been anything appealing promised on the cover, feeling extravagant having money in my pocket for the first time in a week. Driving the Jeep makes me feel great and at a traffic light pull up beside two young women in a Mercedes. They both look at me, turn to each other and look back at me. I play hard to get (dumb) keeping them in sight behind me as we're driving up Route 1. I lose them and end up behind two motorcycle guys the whole rest of the way to Madison. Back home, after dinner, Bernadette asks if I've noticed a vacuum cleaner anywhere. More getting-ready-to-leave stuff. Stephanie came by while I was out and left word for me to clean the stall, which I did right after cleaning up after dinner. Two wheelbarrows full of shit and dirt which she had gathered. We can't get hold of a blacksmith to come and replace a shoe that Sean has lost. That's been the biggest crisis since we've been here besides running out of money, the big car's radiator getting worse and worse, the outside hose nozzle mysteriously quitting working and wondering for a day or two whether Lewis' postcard to Rackstraw Downes, letting him know that his cover was received and sent off to the publisher, ever got mailed. That riddle was answered yesterday with the arrival of a postcard from Rackstraw letting Lewis know that his first postcard was indeed received. No one's gotten enough mail, even supplemented with Maureen's and Ted's magazines and circulars arriving. So now Bernadette, Lewis and I have just watched *Cape Fear* with Robert Mitchum playing a totally bad guy terrorizing the upstanding solid citizen Gregory Peck and his faithful wife Polly Bergen. I fell asleep for a while and missed some of the buildup final tension, but woke in time for the final hand-to-hand combat, Mitchum the animal with no shirt subdued by Peck who restrains himself from killing him to put him back in a cage for some of his own medicine, make him sweat out the days and minutes till he rots. Bernadette and I had agreed to watch it this afternoon with Lewis who assured us it was great and necessary in our lives. Before it went on we'd all been sitting in the dining room having a great conversation about the origins of our names. Bernadette had been looking them up in the *OED*. We are finding out the genealogy of Bernadette's family when Lewis mentioned the magic word 'ice cream,' so I, after three glasses of wine, well on my way to getting loose, volunteered to go to Friendly's to pick some up. The empty streets provoked me again, the way they did a few weeks ago when I was driving around at night after a few beers. It led me to do the same thing, which was drive fast (even dumber). Friendly's was the same repugnant scene, some mother with fake eyelashes hugging her son who seemed old enough to not allow her to do it right in front of everybody. She knocked into me with her purse without excusing herself.

July 18

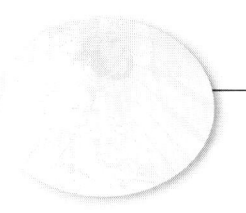

Dreamt there was an elephant guarding us at Cape Fear, I think, it was a skinny, funny looking elephant. Then Lewis's birthday party a huge occasion during which: John Cage tap dances around the rooms, I unpack and find everything I ever lost in the world, I put a lot of old clothes away, Lewis and I reassess our lives, chocolate is served in big chunks kept in ice cold water in a bathtub, a (foreign) person asks me for water from the third well (he says it will be sweeter than any other), but since he has such a strong accent I cannot for a long time understand what he's trying to say, a performance of Wagner is being put on outside in velvet pools but somehow it is actually "Swan Lake" as a Wagnerian opera, then as we try to watch it we see a kidnapping taking place to the tune of "The Green, Green Grass of Home," and the kidnappers inanely follow the directions of the song (because the song inanely says "the grass is greener on the other side of the fence") so they or we have to stay off of it and the kidnapping is prevented (like the plot of *Cape Fear*), then I walk backwards for a long time. When I woke up it was late, Lewis and I had made a deal that he'd get up with the children this morning if I'd watch the movie with him last night, and we ate ice cream, aluminum ice cream from Friendly's as I referred to it ten years ago. I ate a pear and cleaned the upstairs. Greg took Marie and Sophie to the playground across the road and Lewis and Max and I went to do the shopping for the things we've used up ("The Man That Was Used Up" by E.A. Poe). We secretly ate some pizza at the shopping center because we are so tired of fixing food. Greg had taken our journals to be Xeroxed, along with some pages from one of the utopian books. The supermarket was crowded and when we got on line there was a woman before us who bought $128 worth of food, including all sorts of things like Strawberry Pop-Tarts and Fudgesicles and heaps of old raw meat and Weight Watcher's milk whatever that is and frozen dinners and Vienna Fingers, she didn't have one good thing. So it took us a long time. When we got back Greg, Marie and Sophia were lying around reading and drawing and had been to a marsh where Greg lost his glasses while he was chasing Sophia and he couldn't find them. Marie tells proudly that she did. Greg seems real relaxed and happy but we're all feeling horrible about leaving. Lewis still wants to leave tomorrow to save everyone the trouble of having 11 people in the house, so we still don't have a plan. It was a great pleasure to try to make the house look pristine. We went then to the Sound for one last time, there were a lot of cars in the parking lot. We walked onto the beach, Stephanie came up to us with her father, Quincy Howe, a trim man with a weak but friendly smile. We introduced all around and grinned. Most of the people on the beach were approaching the water very gingerly and I asked a man (with a beard and a child) about the jellyfish, he said he'd been swimming and didn't notice anything but that he felt itchy afterwards. Another man at the edge of the delineated swimming area was pushing a jellyfish to the shore to beach it. I decided to jump in and swam around as fast as I could, I'd had such a great desire to feel the salt water again and it was so buoyant and wonderful, afterwards I felt itchy but I don't think I was stung. A boy got stung while we were there and another man – these self-appointed guardians of society – began collecting jellyfish in a pail, spiriting them in with a shovel and when we looked twice we realized it was our pail and shovel. Then he dug a hole and buried them just like those boys we had seen before, believing them to be sadists, I guess this is just a tradition, neither harsh nor not. By this time nobody at all was swimming and I decided to tell the kids not to go in the water. We played in the playground, sat for a while looking at the sea and went home. We had soup and I felt disjointed and confused. While nursing Max and (Marx!) then afterwards sitting in the old outdoor chair, I finished reading Greg's journal which is full of long headlong wavelike sentences which made me envious and long descriptions and it's obvious when Greg is in the outdoors he is more there than I am always in my head. Also there's so many things we don't say, both of us, because our audience is prearranged, it's Greg and me, Lewis, Maureen and Ted. So we leave out some things. I know I do but one way or another I'm ashamed of myself anyway. I went outside for what might be my last look for a while at the Owen and Mankovich greenery at evening and found myself thinking of how women try to please men in the world and do treat them in their minds as figures of authority often from their fathers, and of Greg's reactions to our life with our children which I believe to be quite accurate – one doesn't have children to lessen one's narcissism I hope, I assume the reason for having them is to propagate the race, though often one has them because one fucks and gets pregnant, but then the children become overweening and one caters to them excessively because of one's excessive narcissism, inevitably (I almost typed executive narcissism) which is not exactly news to me, I always assumed there should be some community or communal arrangement for children focused at the very least on meals and schools, but why am I going into all this now? Greg has just come in with today's journal, this is very like a newspaper office. I'd just like to add that I can't understand why men (who feel free to imply that there is a way to be that they enjoy perhaps better than some other) don't clean bathrooms, and often are not interested in cooking even when it's obvious that everyone is hungry. But I don't want to end there, I'll have to say something else. Tomorrow, like a line from another Edgar Allan Poe story I can remember, I may be gone from this world completely and at odds and at a loss again and maybe even angry again in my tightened little city which seems not to exist yet. Greg is photographing us.

    Books read by Lewis this month:
    How German Is It, Walter Abish
    Extremities, Rae Armantrout
    Neurotic Styles, David Shapiro (another one)
    Light in August, William Faulkner
    Appointment in Samarra John O'Hara
    All My Friends are Going to be Strangers, Larry McMurtry
    Rimbaud
    Mayakovsky
    Wallace Stevens
    Ghosts, Ed McBain
    The Eagle's Gift, Carlos Castaneda
    City Police
    Second Sex, Simone de Beauvoir
    Various art books
    New Blood
    Two Suspicious Girls, Katie Mitchell [Katie Schneeman and Tessa Mitchell]
    Remembering Gurdjieff, Fritz Peters

July 18

Xeroxed both mine and Bernadette's journals this afternoon and put them together with a cover and illustrations by Marie as a gift for Maureen and Ted to show them we've made productive use of their home. I didn't think I'd write any more (this afternoon on the beach Bernadette said I was over-journalized because I commented that Stephanie's father's belly button seemed to be off center). We went for the same walk earlier in the day with Marie and Sophie that I'd gone on with Marie last night so that Lewis and Bernadette could continue cleaning the house and go shopping to replenish all the items we'd used up of Ted and Maureen's, Bernadette had a list. The most adventurous part of the walk, going off into the wild on some almost obscure path, was thwarted when Sophie refused to come along and I lost my eyeglasses rushing back to find her because she didn't answer my calls and I was terrified she walked off somewhere. It took Marie and I what seemed like a long time to find them. And then I wasn't in such a good mood the rest of the walk, kind of walking ahead and letting them be with themselves. It was incredibly hot too. All I wanted to do was to be in the cool living room listening to records. After dinner, we read each other's journals. Bernadette can be so concise and exact in this offhand, casual way where she's observing something and then reports it with her friendly speech which can get to be a long written sentence but isn't any different from the way she'd speak. And I also like the way she writes about frustration and anger. This is the last night of our retreat. I feel called on to make an assessment, but it's all in here. What I've been looking forward to doing is putting the following list in:

Books read:

Agnes and Sally, Lewis Warsh (in mss.)
Leaving Cheyenne, Larry McMurtry
Story of an African Farm, Olive Schreiner
Appointment in Samarra, John O'Hara
Drastic Measures, Pat Nolan
Summer Sleeper, Sandy Berrigan
Mythologizing Always, Pat Jones
Disfrutes, Charles Bernstein
Coming Into the Country, John McPhee
Things I Didn't Know I Loved, Nazim Hikmet
Reveries of the Solitary Walker, Jean-Jacques Rousseau
All My Friends are Going to be Strangers, Larry McMurtry
Sound and the Fury and *As I Lay Dying*, William Faulkner
The Congresswoman, Aristophanes

Eels on toast points

one two three o'clock four o'clock rock
cloche de tenebrous fumes a heat wave
is starting a new school of poetry in
this messy always non-utopic universe
of money and pleasure without any measure

sweet old times this is no real regimen
si usted desea que su nombre aparezca
en la lista de oradores, favor de llamar
a Bernadette Mayer antes del mediodia de
1981 but always I will be nice to you

you are my hidden utopian pleasure there
is no satire in my attitude to you or
my giving you the inane qualities as a moth
writing these workers poems identical to
the squeezing of the pig in a certain month

you walk in and out the door and up and down
the stairs till you're permitted to retire
to one of the wider beds in the upstairs
where we could actually all fit and fuck
if none of us was proprietary at all

unless it's more pleasure not to fuck together
and easier to earn money that way, no having
to make the unsaid tedium of own corporations
like boring socialism even in the fucking bed
she said you know the thing I love's to be alone

so leave me go I am a mind or of one to become
all gone or all alone in your house without you
& it's because I love you and love to play tunes
on your excised double-decker flute like a face
before which almost any kind of music is nowhere

[BM]

Who Am I? Forgive Me

An ugly little monster is born in Connecticut
bursting out of a man's heart after dinner
it grows up housed in the spaceship's corridors
to be a combination shark, machine and Godzilla
till it destroys everybody who's looked expectantly
around the corners of the place for its forms
(including the scientist who's a robot who gets
his head knocked off and inside it's milk and wires)
except for this handsome woman who gregariously
masters and ejects the thing from the emergency
shuttle then she puts herself to sleep by freezing
till somebody will be able to pick her up later
with the cat, we watched all that and you walked
into the file cabinet again gashing your leg
which is my head and closer to your heart but
it wasn't serious and the country's hot
and full of movies including *American Gigolo*
no real sex scenes just these shots of legs
with hands on them with a kind of tittering
music behind and between the three faces of the man
and woman of your body with torso and sex-eyes
are the crooked stiles and disproportions of poems
contraptions distracting a crooked man like Stesichorus
from earth human being who brings along her harpsichord
I to dance on water and sing choruses with Terpsichore
muse of the way you go up and down the corner.

[BM]

Waiting for Maureen

The clothesline in a final dusk's got
a bright Batman beach blanket and
a pair of cut-offs. On the littered
table at which I sit, some Queen Anne's Lace
in a bottle of water, a dead fly at the bottom.
The colored bird calls, the bowed crickets, a lone
airplane, the TV in the next room, two kids
giggling calm before sleep through wood, what to
call a journal work before its Medici gets back.
Cats in the wind, lilies, lanterns, cows and whiskey.
Sneakers snug down on my feet, a lit cigarette,
flies, a screen door, her five-year-old breathing.
Green sand, stars of our own backyard and supper club.
Dead skunk at the side of the road, blatant neighbors.
The jewel of our living together at the pharmacy
getting developed, a slow rabbit.

[GM]

(Guilford, Connecticut, June 21-July 18, 1981)

Visitors included:

Barbara Barg, poet; author of *Obeying the Chemicals (Hard Press); The Origin of the Species* (Semiotext(e)/Native Agents); member of Homer Erotic; editor/co-publisher of Power Mad Books

Chris Bobin, quilt maker, shown at Union Square Gallery

Joel Chassler, philosophical cartoonist; editor, Power Mad Press

Peggy de Coursey, explorer

Cynthia Hedstrom, dancer, choreographer, director of Danspace

Susan (Suki) Howe, poet, author of *My Emily Dickinson*

Steve Levine, poet; author of *To and For* (Coffee House, 1992); editor/co-publisher of Power Mad Books

Rose Lesniak, poet; founder and president of Out There Productions; member of P.O.E.T. (Poets Overland Expeditionary Troop); now a dog trainer in Miami

Grace Murphy, friend

Michael Scholnick, poet; co-editor of *Mag City;* author of *Clinch: Selected Poems* (Coffee House, 1998)